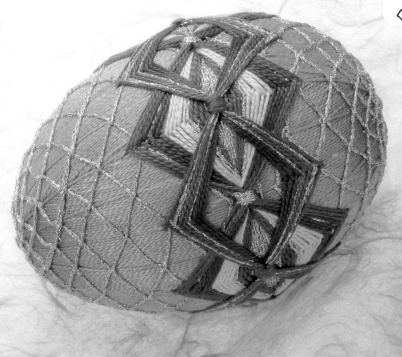

Princess's Crown *P.104*

Columbine *P.65*

Garland of Ribbons *P.88*

Friendship Chain *P.43*

Chrysanthemum *P.97*

Spinning Top *P.82*

Wishing Papers *P.74*

Rippling River *P.117*

Contents

Introduction
—— a history of Temari ——

Because information in English about Temari is extremely limited, the history that is supplied here stems from many different perspectives.

The origins of Temari may have been in China. In China, the decorated ball is a symbol commonly used in conjunction with the lion. Two stone lions frequently guard the gates of official buildings for the purpose of demonscaring and protection. The male lion, on one side of the gate, usually has his front paw on a patterned ball, the lioness, on the other side, is portrayed with her cub. Another common Chinese symbol shows two lions playing with an ornately patterned ball which perhaps has a similar significance to two dragons fighting for the flaming pearl of supremacy. No lions are indigenious to China and, because they are generally shown playing with a ball, this seems to show that they are considered to be mythical animals, good-natured and playful, not fierce and ominous like the tiger.

A favorite theatrical amusement of the Chinese is called "Exercising the Lions" or "Shua Shih Tzu," a ceremonial dance again for the purpose of expelling demons. Two men dance in the front and back halves of the lion costume, coordinating their movements with extraordinary agility. A third man tempts and teases the lion with an enormous decorated ball. The ball represents the sun, the egg symbol of the dual powers of nature — "yin and yang," and at the same time, a precious stone, the flaming pearl, which symbollizes profound treasure and happiness.

An ancient legend tells that the mythical lion produces milk from its paws, and so hollow but brightly decorated balls were placed in the hills by the country people. It was hoped that the lions, while playing with the balls, would leave some of their milk inside, which the people could then collect and use for its magical powers.

As a toy in Japan, it is believed that Temari or "hand ball" began as *Kemari* or literally "kick ball." Kemari was a game introduced from China around the 7th century A.D. and is one of the oldest sports known in Japan, though it is played there no longer. The game was played by four, six or eight persons kicking a deer skin ball that resembled two thick hamburger buns joined together with a heavy seam. The participants kicked the ball in turn, trying to keep it from touching the ground or going out of the three meter (ten foot) square playing field. In each of the four corners of the field a different kind of tree was planted: pine, willow, maple and cherry. The purpose of the game was not only for the players to make high scores by repeatedly kicking the ball high in the air but also to display elegant and graceful form in kicking. Customarily the winning player was presented with a gift or bouquet of flowers, the loser was taunted and ridiculed by the spectators.

Kemari was played in the Emperor's court from around the 8th century and reached the peak of its popularity between the 11th and 13th centuries. At that time skill in the game was considered as much a requisite for a nobleman's elegance as his ability to write poetry. It is said that Kemari was not popular among the *Samurai*, the elite military class, because of their ultra-conservative self-discipline and their stoic philosophy of living. The game to them was considered frivolous. During the Edo Period (1603—1867) it became fashionable among the trading classes. A form of the game still exists today in Korea, and right now in the United States, the game of "Hacky Sack," played by teen-age boys for soccer practice with a small sand-filled leather ball, is a direct descendent of Kemari.

Temari or "hand ball" was undoubtedly a toy invented for the amusement of young boys and girls of the wealthy nobility. They were made from salvaged silk fabric scraps and threads unravelled from discarded kimonos. At first the balls were tossed from one to another as a game of catch. After the 15th century with the introduction of cotton cultivation into Japan, Temari began to be stuffed with cotton and wrapped with cotton yarn. Because cotton was fairly inexpensive and widely available, Temari, now called *"Ito-Mari"* or "thread-ball," began to have plebian or common life and its popularity spread quickly. It is said that during the Edo Period between the 17th and 19th centuries, Temari became beautiful, wrapped in colorful threads that were arranged in a variety of bright designs. And during this period many different ways of playing with Temari developed. With the invention of cotton Temari, the game of ball changed from essentially a game of catch to bouncing the balls in the ground.

Until the early 1600's, the ball games were played outdoors, with participants standing up. But during that time, the time of the famous *Shogun Tokugawa*, widespread warfare between clans of different feudal principalities made any outdoor play unsafe, so young girls of the nobility and affluent classes were made to play indoors, safe behind the confines of castle walls. Thus the game changed and was popularly played by bouncing the balls on the floor in a kneeling position while chanting a *"Temari-Uta."* These were nonsense songs similar to our jump rope rhymes, made up by children and usually meaningless, a typical "Temari-Uta" sounds like this:

> "To *Inari-san* on the side lane,
>   I offered one *sen* and, quickly worshipping,
>   Hurried to *Osen's* teahouse;
>   As I sat down a cup of tea was brought;
>   Looked sideways at the tea,
>   Mud-cakes or rice-cakes;
>   There I won one count."

It was perhaps during this time that the *"Otedama"* or beanbag games developed. A cousin of Temari, the beanbags were also made of scraps of colored cloth which were often brightly embroidered and filled with red *azuki* beans or rice. They were spherical in shape and made small enough to fit into a child's hand. Some had bells attached or included inside the filling. Today we find Temari whose cores are filled with a variety of materials including sand, crushed clam shells, paper and rice. Often times modern day Temari include a bell inside the central core.

In some areas of Japan, balls are stuffed with a central core of tightly crumpled paper or wadded fabric and wrapped with cotton cloth strips, then finish with a colored-thread embroidery pattern. These are called *"Goten-Mari."*

With the Meiji Era (1868—1912) came the introduction of rubber into Japan. *"Gomu-Mari"* or rubber balls became instantly popular for games-playing. At this point in the progression of modern industrialization many a handicraft the world over has become extinct. But because of the beloved tradition and beauty associated with the thread balls, Temari has been perpetuated in its ancient form until today.

Prior to mass-media communication, the patterns, styles and colors of Temari were regional within geographic areas of Japan, often following the customs and symbols of the district. Patterns were frequently derived from nature, many having the names of flowers, such as *"Kiku"* (chrysanthemum), *"Ume"* (plum blossom), or *"Botan"* (peony), while others have been named for patterns in nature that they might resemble, such as pine needles, shimmering streams, shooting stars, fireworks, ocean waves and fish nets. Complex geometric designs of interlocking squares, triangles, diamonds and pentagons provide another range of design categories.

Since World War II, a rekindling of interest in the art of Temari has been taking place in Japan and has spread energetically to the United States. Temari societies now exist in Japan through which new designs are being created, registered and shared. Students of Temari are rewarded for their skills and are presented with certificates of expertise on four graduating levels: Novice, Advanced, Teacher and Master, each signifying many hours of meticulous work and skillful creativity.

Traditionally Temari have been made by mothers and grandmothers for their young daughters as a New Year's gift. As the end of the old year draws near, the mother secretly begins winding a ball and planning its decorative pattern. When New Year's Day dawns and the daughter awakens, next to her pillow lies a new Temari of exquisite color and design.

The author's first experience with Temari came with the arrival of the son of our "Japanese family" and his new bride on a visit to our home in Santa Barbara as part of their honeymoon trip. The bride presented my father, my mother and I each with an exquisite embroidered ball. Made by the bride's mother, each had its own unique designs and colors and an elaborate tassel and dragonfly knot. These auspicious gifts, made of time and patience and love and joy, were presented to my family with humble thanks offered for gracious hospitality. Needless to say, this stirred great emotion in the three of us. And it ignited my curiosity and eventual affection for the tradition of Temari, a very special gift to be given with very special love.

How to use this book

Before you begin, read "Materials for Wrapping the Ball" for an explanation of what is needed (pages 19 to 20). Then read through the instructions for "Wrapping the Ball," "Dividing the Ball," and "Marking the Ball" as an introduction to what is to come (pages 21 to 35).

The instructions in this book are presented in the order that they are meant to be completed. The temari designs are presented in order from the simplest to gradually more complex. Each ball introduces a few innovations that will be used in successive balls. Many materials are repeated from one ball to the next. Thread colors are often used in several designs.

Overview for Wrapping, Dividing and Marking the Ball:

1. Each ball is wrapped with three layers of different materials as a base for stitching.
2. The surface of each ball is divided into equal parts as a basis for the decorative pattern using a paper tape measure and pins.
3. The resultant divisions on each ball are simply marked with thread of a contrasting color and used as guidelines for the pattern.
   These steps are preliminary before every ball is decorated. They are simple procedures that can be accomplished quickly. The beginning page for each design gives further instructions for dividing and marking along with a list of materials. The first list of materials includes everything that is needed to complete Ball #1 "The Learning Ball."

Materials for Wrapping the Balls

All of the materials selected for use in this book have been chosen for their accessibility. In some cases brand names have been suggested in order to more specifically describe a material. In the case of the Pearl Cotton #5, DMC has been used exclusively for the projects in this book because of its wide range of colors and its keying abilities. For all of the materials listed, a generic description is provided for clarification, as well as the type of shop where the material can be purchased.

Styrofoam Balls and Eggs—found in hobby or craft stores, the measurement size refers to the diameter of the ball, i.e. a 3 inch ball measures 3 inches through the center of the ball, not around the outside of the ball. The measurement of the egg is from top to bottom through its center, not around the outside. Check each styrofoam blank carefully before you buy to make sure there are no dents or flat spots on the surface; these may cause difficulty when the marking process begins.

Polyester Batting also called Fleece—found in fabric stores, is 1/4 to 3/8 inch or 1/2 to 1 centimeter thick. It is commonly used for trapunto and applique, has low loft with consistent texture and thickness throughout. Batting can be purchased by the yard from a bolt or can be found pre-cut in a plastic bag.

The Yarn Wrap can be any inexpensive or left over 2 ply or 3 ply baby, sock or sport yarn of consistent texture. Finer, light weight yarns are preferrable, heavier weight yarns create lumps on the ball's surface. The yarn's color should be a similar shade to the outer thread wrap. The closer the shade, the easier to wrap the outer thread wrap. If you are without yarn of a similar color to the outer thread wrap, use yarn of a similar value, i.e. white under pastel colors, black, brown or navy under deeper shades. Look for wrapping yarns in discount yarn outlets. Often mill ends and odd lots are just what you need. Fiber content doesn't matter.

The Thread Wrap—regular sewing thread of any brand is perfect for the outer thread wrap. It can be polyester or all cotton. The variety of colors is wonderful. But remember: select your Pearl Cotton #5 decorative threads first, then match the sewing thread to them. It takes approximately 250 yards of sewing thread to cover a 3 inch ball for the outer thread wrap. Check the yardage on the spool to make sure there is enough. Two small spools or one medium spool of thread will cover a 3 inch ball. One large spool of thread or one medium and one small spool will cover a 4 inch styrofoam ball.

Single Filament Metallic Thread is commonly used for machine embroidery. It can be found in fabric stores and is wrapped on spools similar to regular sewing thread. This thread is NOT HEAVY ENOUGH to use FOR MARKING THREAD. It is used only to add more glitter to the ball's surface over the thread wrap.

Needles—temari requires a long sharp needle with a large eye. "Cotton Darners" most closely approximate Japanese temari needles and may be found in fabric stores. One yarn needle is helpful for using to secure the yarn wrap end.

Glass-Headed Pins should be 1-1/4 inches in length and come in a variety of 6 to 8 different colors; purchased in fabric stores.

Red Tomato Pincushion—upon which colored glass-headed pins are separated according to color.

Fabric Shears—for cutting polyester batting for the balls and cheesecloth for the eggs, the sharper the better.

Thread Scissors—small needlework scissors with sharp points for cutting single threads.

Centimeter Tape Measure—the common wind-up variety that measures 150 centimeters on one side of the tape and 60 inches on the backside. The smaller the better.

Measuring Papers—the best paper for 3 inch balls is ordinary 8-1/2 by 11 inch bond typing paper or paper used in photo-copying machines. Cut the paper lengthwise into strips that measure 3/8 inch or 1 centimeter wide by 11 inches long. Use a paper cutter for best results, and cut a large number at once. For larger balls, over 3 inches in diameter, use quilling paper. It can be found in most hobby and craft shops and is already cut into long length strips. Newsprint and tissue are too flimsy to be used for measuring papers.

Tissue Paper—for use in the wide *obi* patterns, refers to the common type used to wrap clothing. Use only white paper, dyed papers could stain your ball. The Japanese actually use rice paper for this.

Circular Paper Patterns are used to cut the batting to fit different sized balls. To cut the circles, use newsprint or any large scrap paper. With your tape measure, find the circumference (length around the ball), this measurement plus 1/2 inch will be the DIAMETER or width of the circle pattern. Divide the diameter in HALF and this will give you the center of the circle. If you don't have a compass draw the pattern by tying a piece of string around your pencil with the other end tied around a pin at the circle's center. Pull the pencil taut at the end of the string and draw the circle around the center pin.

Gold and Silver Metallic Marking Thread—for dividing the ball, generically these are called "knitting metallics" or "needlepoint/stitchery metallics." They can be found in larger yarn and needlecraft stores. Threads should be 6 to 10 strands, 8 strands is ideal. They should be twisted, not chained or wrapped. Fiber content is commonly 65% Viscose and 35% Polyester.
Some companies that produce excellent metallics that are ideal for *Temari* are Welcomme's "L'Esquisse," Phildar's "Sunset 330," Anni Blatt, Balger and Madeira. Most are made in France, Germany or Japan.

Surface Decoration Threads—known as Pearl Cotton #5 weight. Many companies make #5 weight needlecraft threads. DMC is commonly accessible, has a huge variety of hues and shades and provides ease in keying or coordinating colors and shades. Two skeins of DMC thread almost equal one ball of thread. To prepare skeined threads, wrap them around a 2 by 3 inch piece of stiff cardboard. Write the color number and manufacturer name on the cardboard for future reference. Purchase Pearl Cotton #5 in your needlecraft store.

Transparent Nylon Thread or black regular sewing thread can be used to make hanging loops for balls. Purchase either type in fabric stores.

Cheesecloth for Faberge eggs, #60 grade cotton gauze is a tightly woven weight of gauze that simulates the thread wrap layer on a ball. Gauze or cheesecloth may be purchased at fabric stores by the yard.

Wrapping the Ball

WHY: By wrapping the ball with three layers of material; batting over the styrofoam, yarn over the batting layer, and thread over the yarn layer, the ball is given a firm foundation upon which the design layer can be easily stitched. (Fig. 1)

1. The styrofoam ball provides an accurate spherical core. It is light weight and provides a convenient foundation over which the three materials are applied. In Japan, instead of the styrofoam ball, a piece of plastic, paper or fabric is wadded up and then wrapped over. It is difficult to make these materials accurately spherical.
2. The batting layer covers the styrofoam ball and allows for padding over the styrofoam core. It gives added thickness through which to sew.
3. The yarn layer provides coverage quickly and cheaply for the white batting layer and a smooth firm foundation for the thread layer.
4. The outer thread layer provides a refined background on top of which the design embroidery is applied. The sewing thread used for this layer provides an unlimited variety of colors. The thin texture of the thread allows tiny fine stitches to be taken while embroidering the pattern.

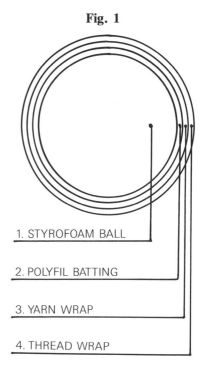

Fig. 1

1. STYROFOAM BALL

2. POLYFIL BATTING

3. YARN WRAP

4. THREAD WRAP

MATERIALS:

One 3 inch diameter styrofoam ball

Polyester batting, approximately 1/4 to 3/8 inch or 1/2 to 1 centimeter thickness

Glass-headed pins in a variety of colors, about 1-1/4 inches length

Scissors, medium-sized and sharp

2 or 3 ply yarn, white or black or a color that will disappear behind or blend with outer thread wrap color, 1 skein. For Ball #1, something that will coordinate with RED thread wrap.

#50 sewing thread, 250 yards or 2 small spools — see "Materials for Wrapping the Ball" (page 19) for amount/spool sizes. Refer to the first page of each chapter for thread wrap color. Ball #1 uses bright red.

Centimeter tape measure

Compass, Pencil, Paper

METHOD:

THE BATTING LAYER

1. Measure around the styrofoam ball (circumference).
   (Fig. 2)

2. From the batting, cut a circle whose diameter equals the circumference of the styrofoam ball:
   (Fig. 3)
   A. Measure the ball's circumference add 1/2 inch
   B. Divide the circumference in half
   C. Use this half as radius of batting circle
   D. Using a compass, draw a circular paper pattern with above radius
   E. Cut batting circle from paper pattern
   F. Save the paper pattern

Fig. 2

Fig. 4

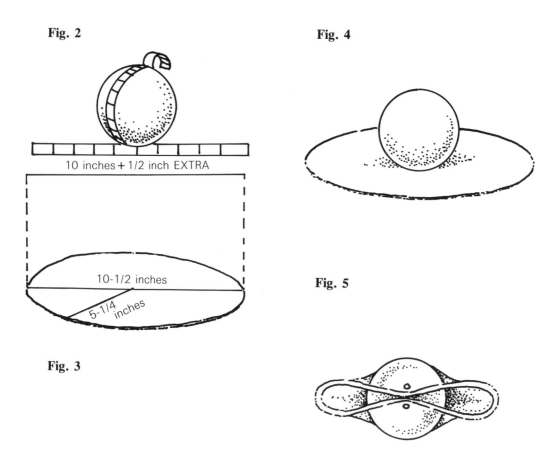

10 inches + 1/2 inch EXTRA

10-1/2 inches

5-1/4 inches

Fig. 5

Fig. 3

3. Place the styrofoam ball in the center of the batting circle. (Fig. 4)

4. Mold up 2 opposite sides of the circle to the top of the ball.
   Place a pin on each side about 1/2 inch from the center. (Fig. 5)

5. Equally divide the 2 loops, making them into quarters. Mold up and pin to the ball. (Fig. 6)

6. Divide each quarter into half and pin to make 8 equal loops at the top. (Fig. 7)

   ** BE SURE THE BATTING IS MOLDED SMOOTHLY AND EVENLY ON THE BALL WITH NO
   WRINKLES.

Fig. 6

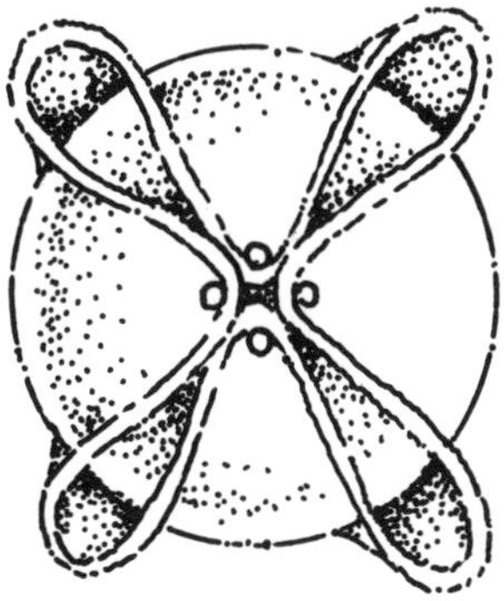

Fig. 7

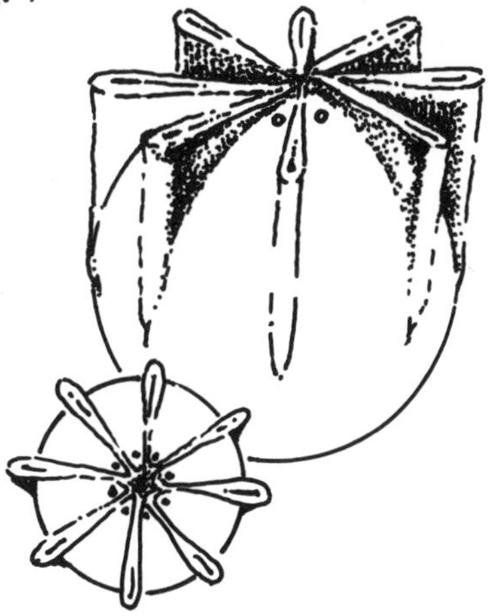

Fig. 8

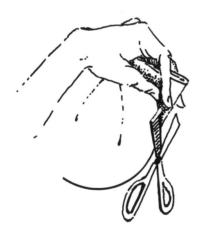

7. Starting around the circle, with the fingers of the
   left hand, pinch loop into a flat fold. With right
   hand, use scissors to cut excess off the surface of
   the ball. (Figs. 8 and 9)

   Do not cut too closely so as to leave gaps in the
   batting cover.

   Do not leave overlap of excess, it will cause
   lumps.

Fig. 9

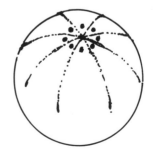

We now have a tailor-made batting cover for the ball.

23

THE YARN LAYER

1. Leave the 8 pins in place.

2. Using the 3-ply yarn, begin to wrap the yarn around the ball as you would wind a ball of yarn, BUT CHANGE THE POSITION OF THE BALL EACH TIME YOU TAKE THE YARN AROUND. THREADS MUST NOT LINE UP 3—4 ON TOP OF EACH OTHER. (Fig. 10)

3. After several turns of yarn over the batting layer, remove all 8 pins.

4. Continue to wrap the ball smoothly until the white batting has disappeared. Try to keep even tension on the yarn while wrapping. If the yarn is pulled too tightly over the ball, lumps can occur.

5. Keep pressing the surface of the ball together with the palms of both hands to keep it smooth.

6. Use the eye-end of the needle to move around some of the yarn's threads and help cover up white spots of batting and holes in the wrap layer.

7. Anchor the yarn by threading it into a needle and taking 2—3 large stitches into the surface. (Fig. 11)

8. Cut off yarn end close to the surface of the ball.

Fig. 10   **Fig. 11**

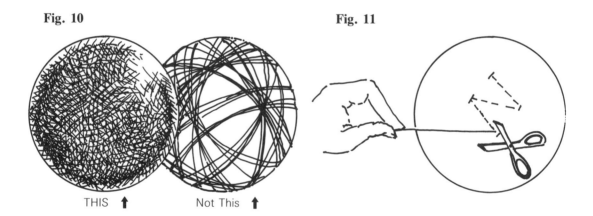

THIS ↑   Not This ↑

THE THREAD LAYER

1. Using the #50 sewing thread, wrap the outer thread layer onto the ball.

   ** KEEP TURNING THE BALL SO THAT THREADS are evenly distributed. DO NOT LINE UP 3—4 ON TOP OF EACH OTHER in the same line. (Fig. 10)

   ** WRAP THE THREAD SO THAT IT GOES AROUND THE CENTER OF THE BALL EACH TIME, NOT AROUND THE SIDES SO THAT IT CAN SLIP OFF.

2. Continue wrapping until the thread layer completely covers the yarn layer. Again use the eye-end of the needle to help pull threads over holes.

3. To anchor the thread when the wrap is complete, cut the thread, thread the end into a needle and take 2—3 zigzagging stitches into the ball. Pull the thread taut and cut it down at the ball's surface.
   (Fig. 11)

EXTRAS:

Metallic Thread: Over the thread layer may be sparsely wrapped a fine single-filament metallic thread to add glitter to the ball. See "Materials for Wrapping the Ball" (page 19) for a description.

It is not necessary to add this glitter layer to every ball.

To put a bell inside:

Often a small bell or noisemaking object is included inside the styrofoam core. In order for the object to make a sound it must be enclosed in a small box. This box can be constructed of cardboard (Fig. 12), or even 2 metal bottle caps or screw-on bottle tops taped together with a small pebble or button inside. Use your imagination! Temari is a craft of invention.

Fig. 12

1 inch

1 inch

1. Take the unwrapped styrofoam ball and, with a ball-point pen, draw a 1-1/2 to 2 inch line onto the ball.

2. Cut the ball in half perpendicular to the line on the ball. Use an electric knife or a serrated bread knife with a sawing motion. (Fig. 13)

Fig. 13

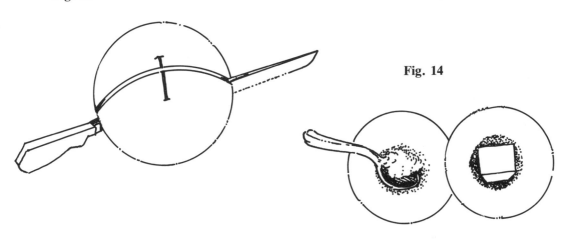

Fig. 14

Fig. 15

3. Use a spoon to scoop out the centers of both halves of the opened ball. Make a hollow space just large enough to accomodate the bell in the box. (Fig. 14)

4. Put the ball back together by matching up the lines made with the ball-point pen.

5. Wrap the two halves tightly with a scrap of yarn. Wind the yarn around the ball several times to anchor the ball into one piece again. (Fig. 15)

6. Proceed with the wrapping process, starting with the batting layer.

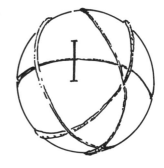

Dividing the Ball

The foundation beneath every temari design, from the simplest to the most complex, is the precise measuring process of the ball's surface.
This determines the ultimate shape of the design.
If the ball is unevenly wrapped, lumpy or lop-sided, the measuring process can be difficult and unnecessarily frustrating.

Before you begin to divide a ball, hold that wrapped ball up to the light, turning it around in all directions and checking its silhouette for bumps.
When you come across a bump, roll it around on a table or flat surface in a circular motion with the palm of one hand.
Make the ball as accurately round as you can before dividing and the dividing will be easier and more accurate. (Fig. 1)

Because we are dealing with a sphere and, in order to clarify instructions, we will use the following terminology:

Fig. 1

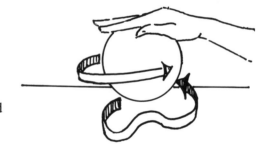

Top — NORTH POLE

Bottom — SOUTH POLE

Middle or Equator — OBI LINE

(The OBI in Japan is a sash or belt worn around the kimono at the waist). (Fig. 2)

OVERVIEW:
Because every ball will be a slightly different size depending upon the wrapping materials and their varied thicknesses, an unmarked paper strip is used as a measuring device.
The paper strip simplifies the measuring process by allowing the circumference of each individual ball to be divided into equal parts simply by folding the strip into halves, fourths, eighths and sixteenths.
It can just as easily be folded into thirds, fifths, sixths, twelfths and so on.

Fig. 2

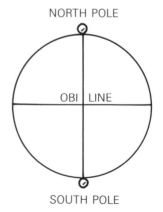

NORTH POLE

OBI LINE

SOUTH POLE

MATERIALS:

One 3 inch diameter styrofoam ball, wrapped in red

2 or 3 paper strips, 3/8 inch wide by 11 inches long. Typing paper works great, newsprint is too flimsy. Strips should be cut straight, with a paper cutter if possible.

Pincushion

Glass-headed pins in a variety of colors. Organize the pins on your pincushion according to color.

Embroidery or thread scissors

Marking thread, medium weight metallic gold for the first ball
   This is an 8—10 strand acetate metallic polyester blend.

Needle, a long sharp needle with a large eye is needed. "Cotton Darners," we've found, most closely approximate Japanese temari needles.

METHOD:

Take the ball. Pin one end of the paper strip to the ball. Pin as close to the end of the strip as possible. This will be the NORTH POLE. With the paper strip, measure around the center of the ball. Come around the ball back to the beginning and mark the strip accurately with a pencil mark or fold line. (Fig. 3)

Fig. 4

Fig. 3

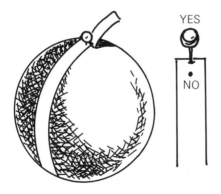

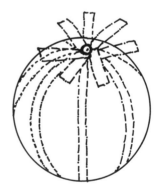

KEEPING THE STRIP PINNED IN PLACE at the NORTH POLE, measure around the ball several times with the strip going in different directions. Check the circumference (length) measurement each time to make sure it is accurate. (Fig. 4)

Fig. 5

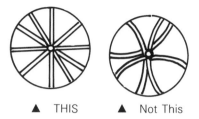

▲ THIS   ▲ Not This

Be sure the strip divides the ball through the center each time you move it. Don't let it slip off sideways. (Fig. 5)

Cut the excess off the strip at your mark. (Fig. 6)

YOU NOW HAVE AN ACCURATE MEASUREMENT OF THE BALL'S CIRCUMFERENCE.

Fig. 6

Fig. 7

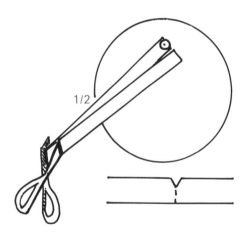

WITHOUT UNPINNING the STRIP, unwrap the strip and fold it carefully in half so that the two ends meet accurately. DON'T UNPIN THE STRIP. (Fig. 7) With your scissors, snip off a tiny corner at the fold line.

Fig. 8

Again wrap the strip around the center of the ball so that the ends come together at the NORTH POLE PIN. Hold the loose end of the strip in place with the left hand. Turn the ball so that the half-notch shows on the bottom. Place a black pin at the center of the notch. This will be the temporary SOUTH POLE. (Fig. 8)

Again wrap the strip around the ball from several
directions starting at the North Pole, gradually adjusting
the placement of the SOUTH POLE PIN.
By doing this 4—5 times from different angles, an
accurate South Pole can be placed.
Check the South Pole's location with the strip several
times from top to bottom. It is important that both Poles
be located accurately opposite each other. (Fig. 9)

Fig. 9

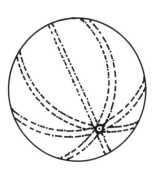

Fig. 10

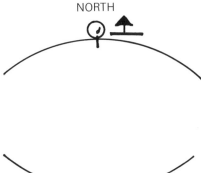

NORTH

SOUTH

NOTE: IN DIAGRAMS, THE NORTH POLE WILL ALWAYS
BE SHOWN AS A WHITE PIN, THE SOUTH POLE
AS A BLACK PIN. (Fig. 10)

STILL, DO NOT REMOVE THE STRIP FROM ITS
ORIGINALLY PINNED POSITION.

Unwrap the loose end of the strip from the ball.
Fold it in half at the notch, and fold it again carefully
into fourths.

Cut a notch at the fold to mark the fourths. (Fig. 11)

Fig. 11

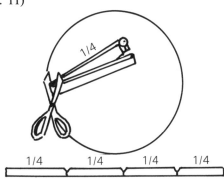

1/4

1/4   1/4   1/4   1/4

TO FIND THE OBI LINE:

Start the paper strip at the North Pole pin.
Divide the ball in half vertically with the strip
between the North and South Poles.
Line up the half-notch at the South Pole pin.
Insert another colored pin at the 1/4 notch.
Do this 6 to 8 times around the ball using
both notches.
Place a pin each time at the 1/4 notches.
(Fig. 12)

Fig. 12

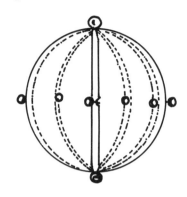

Fig. 13

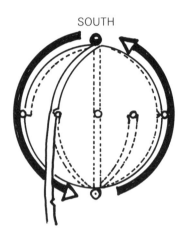

Remove the paper from the North Pole.
Be careful to replace the North Pole pin exactly
in the same place.

Turn the ball so that the South Pole is at the
top. With the paper strip, check each 1/4
mark for accuracy and adjust pins as
necessary. (Fig. 13)
You now have a horizontal line of 12—16 pins
around the equator or OBI LINE of the ball.

TO FIND 8 DIVISIONS AROUND THE OBI LINE (Fig. 14):

Fig. 14

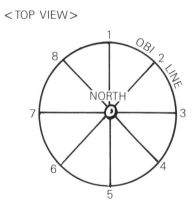

Fig. 15

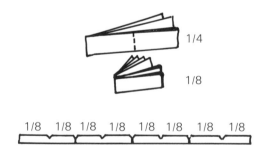

To divide the OBI LINE into 8 (Fig. 15),
USE THE SAME 1/4-NOTCHED PAPER.

First fold your paper strip back into fourths
then fold the fourths in half to make eighths.
Snip a notch at each end to mark the eighths.

Fig. 16

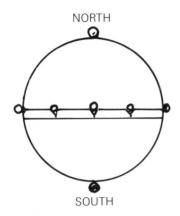

NORTH

SOUTH

Hold your ball with the North Pole at the top. Wrap the paper strip with 1/8 marks around the ball just BELOW the OBI LINE PINS. (Fig. 16)

Fig. 17

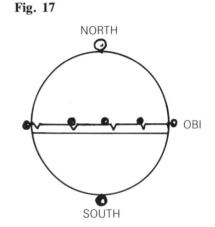

NORTH

OBI

SOUTH

Accurately replace the OBI LINE PINS at the 1/8 notch marks, KEEPING IN LINE WITH YOUR ORIGINAL HORIZONTAL OBI LINE MEASUREMENT. Remove the extra pins. (Fig. 17)

You now have a North Pole, South Pole, and 8 equidistant pins around the Obi Line.

Fig. 18

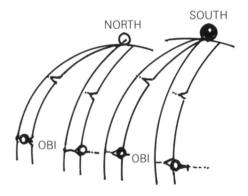

NORTH SOUTH

OBI OBI

Again with your paper strip, use the 1/4 measurement to check the accuracy of your Obi Line. Measure all around, first from the North Pole to the Obi, then from the South Pole to the Obi. (Fig. 18)

THE BALL IS NOW MARKED ONLY WITH PINS, BUT ALL DIVISIONS AND LOCATIONS OF PINS MUST BE AS ACCURATE AS POSSIBLE.

16 DIVISIONS:
More complex balls require more complex divisions. For 16 divisions around the OBI LINE, divide 1/8 section of the SAME PAPER STRIP into half and use it to divide each of the 8 sections around the OBI LINE. Mark each with a pin.

32 DIVISIONS:
Often at this stage a centimeter tape measure becomes easier and more accurate to use. Divide in half each of the 16 sections around the OBI LINE and mark each with a pin.

Marking the Ball

MATERIALS:

Marking thread, 8—10 strand acetate metallic polyester in gold—see "Materials for Wrapping the Ball", or #50 cotton sewing thread in a color to coordinate with the design threads.

(Generally Pearl Cotton #5 is not used for marking the ball because it is too heavy)

Needle, "Cotton Darner"

Embroidery scissors

METHOD: FOR 8 DIVISIONS

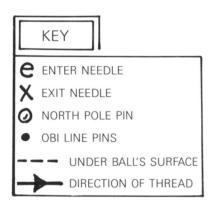

Fig. 1

<TOP VIEW>

8 DIVISIONS

Measure off enough GOLD thread for 4 wraps around the ball plus 5 inches. Thread the needle and knot one thread end. (Fig. 2)

Fig. 2

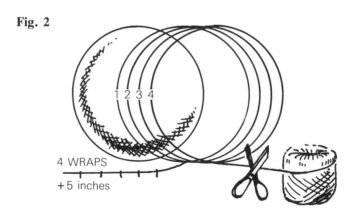

4 WRAPS
+5 inches

Fig. 3

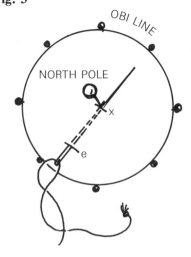

Enter the needle and thread with a long stitch deep beneath the surface of the ball so that the **NEEDLE EXITS EXACTLY AT THE NORTH POLE PIN.** (Fig. 3)

Pull the thread through so that the knot disappears beneath the ball's surface. (Fig. 4)

Fig. 4

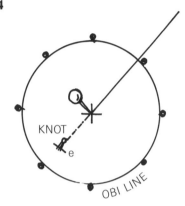

Fig. 5

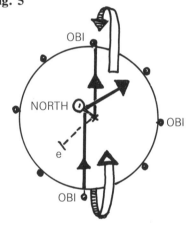

Carry the thread from the NORTH to SOUTH POLE BESIDE ONE OBI LINE PIN, up the opposite side's OBI LINE PIN, back to the NORTH POLE.

Align the thread accurately along side each pin.
Pull the thread taut and hold in place with the fingers of the left hand. (Fig. 5)
DO NOT CUT THE THREAD.

Fig. 6

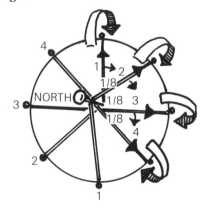

Turn the ball 1/8 of a turn so the thread points to the next OBI LINE PIN. (Fig. 6)
Wrap the thread again to the next OBI LINE PIN, through the SOUTH POLE, to the opposite OBI LINE PIN, and back to the NORTH POLE.

Turn the ball another 1/8 turn and continue to the next OBI LINE PIN. . . and so on around the ball until the 4 wraps are completed.

End the final wrap at the NORTH POLE PIN.

BE SURE THAT ALL 8 THREADS RADIATE ACCURATELY FROM THE CENTER.

Fig. 7

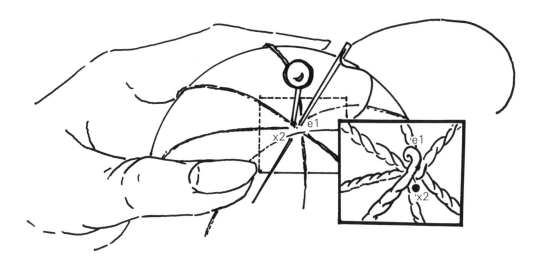

To complete: enter the needle again exactly at the NORTH POLE PIN. (Fig. 7)

Take 3 to 4 tiny stitches to TACK or secure the NORTH POLE THREADS. Be sure to catch the thread turned one quarter around the pin. (Fig. 8)

ESCAPE the thread by entering the needle again through the North Pole and exiting with a long (1 inch) stitch deep beneath the surface threads of the ball like the beginning entrance stitch.

Fig. 8

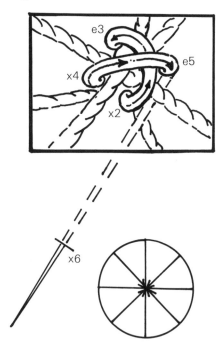

Fig. 9

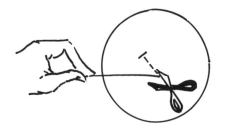

ESCAPE:

Pull the thread through tightly and cut it down at the surface of the ball so that no marking thread shows. (Fig. 9)
BE CAREFUL NOT TO CUT THE WRAPPING THREADS!

As you tacked the North Pole threads with a tiny stitch, TACK THE SOUTH POLE THREADS ALSO.

MARKING THE OBI LINE:

Fig. 10

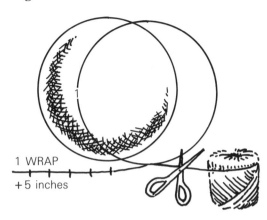

1 WRAP
+5 inches

Measure enough RED SEWING thread for 1 wrap around the ball plus 5 inches. Thread the needle and knot one thread end. (Fig. 10)

This Obi is meant to disappear.

Fig. 11

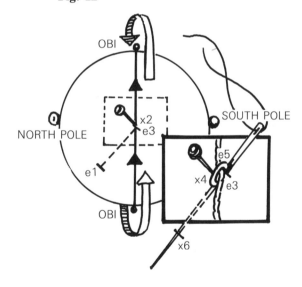

Using one of the OBI LINE PINS the same way the NORTH POLE was used, ENTER the needle about 1 inch away so that the needle EXITS exactly at that OBI LINE PIN. Pull the knot into the ball's surface. (Fig. 11)

Carry the thread around all of the Obi Line pins, aligning it carefully along side each pin.

EXIT the needle at the same point at which you started. Take a tiny TACK stitch to anchor. ESCAPE the thread to the side. (Fig. 12)

Fig. 12

Fig. 13

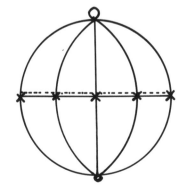

With either #50 sewing thread (for Ball #1 used for the thread wrap) or, for future designs, the gold marking thread, TACK EACH DIVISION INTERSECTION AROUND THE OBI LINE.
This way your measurements will remain accurate. (Fig. 13)

A single tiny cross-stitch over the intersection is sufficient. The thread can be continued from one intersection to the next under the surface of the ball, but this must be done carefully and accurately so measurements do not change.

Selecting the Design Colors

One source tells us that temari were traditionally decorated with five colors. The number five in Japanese culture tied in closely with religious and spiritual beliefs as well as aesthetically and shows up frequently in fine arts and handicrafts. The number five is considered to insure good luck.

Today the range and number of colors used to decorate temari varies widely. Because the selection that is available is so large, color decisions can become difficult to make. Here are some tips:

1. Contrasting colors and values (light and dark) are usually most effective.

2. When choosing colors, keep in mind that you want a light or pastel, a medium, and a dark shade.

3. Variations of the primary colors work well together, for example:

RED	YELLOW	BLUE
Peach	Ecru	Turquoise
Rose	Yellow-green	Blue-violet
Lavendar	Peach	Aqua
Rust	Ivory	Navy

4. Background color (thread wrap) can be a tint (pastel) or shade (dark variation) of one of the colors used. White or black may also be used. Consider which color you want to predominate.

5. Contrast between light and dark values is important to help the design show up.

6. Remember that the marking thread (metallic gold or silver) often is incorporated into the design. Use a metallic or color that will coordinate.

7. If you are having difficulty, ask the shop's salesperson to see the color chart. Color charts are arranged according to keys or ranges of colors. Stay within the color key when selecting tints or shades of the same hue.

Part of the fun of temari is putting the colors together. Experiment, have fun with different combinations. The world of color is yours to enjoy!

BALL #1 "The Learning Ball"

To stitch this ball, we start with the very simplest
Temari design. This design is traditionally used for
teaching the beginning Temari craftsman.

MATERIALS:

One 3 inch styrofoam ball, thread wrap in bright red

DMC Pearl Cotton #5 in 2 colors:
  Yellow #973
  Black #310

Gold marking thread

Paper strip for marking

Optional:
  Single filament gold metallic thread. Over the red
  thread wrap, this single filament gold thread may
  be wrapped sparsely so that spaces in between
  threads are 1/2 to 3/4 inch wide. This adds a little
  more glitter to the ball if desired.
  See "Wrapping the Ball—EXTRAS" (page 25).

Fig. 1

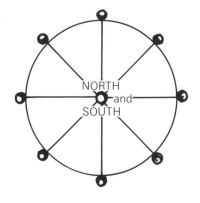

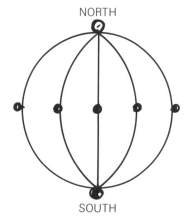

With your paper strip and pins, MEASURE the
ball into EIGHTHS with an OBI MARK. (Fig. 1)

37

Fig. 2

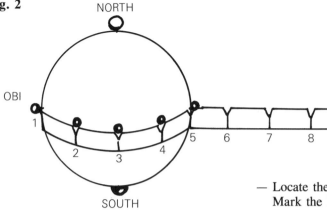

NORTH

OBI

1 2 3 4 5 6 7 8

SOUTH

Fig. 3

<SIDE VIEW>

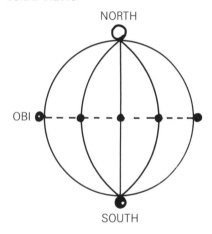

NORTH

OBI

SOUTH

MARK the ball with the GOLD MARKING
THREAD into 8 EQUAL VERTICAL
SECTIONS. Refer to "Marking the Ball"
(page 32) for help.
For this design,
MARK around the OBI LINE, (Fig. 3)
NOT IN GOLD, but in the RED THREAD
WRAP.

TACK the thread intersections at the NORTH
and SOUTH POLES so that they radiate
accurately from the center. (Fig. 4)
TACK the EIGHT DIVISIONS around the
OBI LINE.

TURN the BALL so that the NORTH POLE
FACES YOU. With your paper measure,
divide each of the 8 MARK LINES in HALF
between the NORTH POLE and the OBI line.
(Fig. 5)
Mark each division with a pin.

— Locate the NORTH and SOUTH POLES.
  Mark the North Pole with a WHITE PIN,
  the South Pole with a BLACK PIN.

— Locate the OBI LINE, HALF the distance
  between the NORTH and SOUTH POLES.

— Divide the OBI (or ball's equator) into 8
  EQUAL measurements around the ball.
  MARK EACH with a PIN. (Fig. 2)

Fig. 4

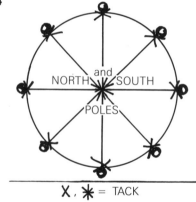

NORTH and SOUTH
POLES

X, ✳ = TACK

Fig. 5

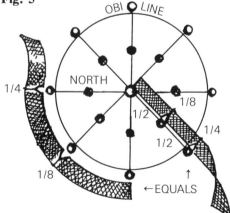

OBI LINE

NORTH

1/4 1/8

1/2

1/2 1/4

1/8 ↑
←EQUALS

38

Fig. 6

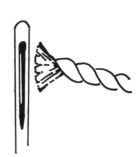

TURN the ball so that the SOUTH POLE FACES YOU. Divide each of the 8 MARK LINES in HALF between the SOUTH POLE and the OBI line. (Fig. 6)
Mark each division with a pin.

Leave all of the MARKING PINS IN PLACE.

THE FOLLOWING STITCH IS THE BASIC STITCH FOR EMBROIDERED TEMARI.

DIRECTIONS for the BASIC STITCH:

Cut a piece of BLACK #310 DMC Pearl Cotton about 4-1/2 feet long.
Thread your needle.

Fig. 7

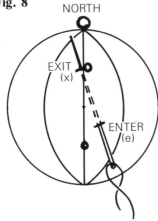

BITE on the very end of the thread with your teeth to flatten it, then stick it through the needle's eye. (Fig. 7)
No knot.

HOLD the ball so that the NORTH POLE is at the TOP.
Near one vertical mark line, ENTER your needle deep into the ball's surface (all the way down into the batting layer) so that it EXITS just to the LEFT of the UPPER 1/2 MARK PIN. (Fig. 8)

Pull the thread through carefully so that the END of the thread DISAPPEARS just beneath the ball's surface. (Fig. 9)

NO KNOT IS NECESSARY if the thread is pulled in very gently to begin.

Fig. 8

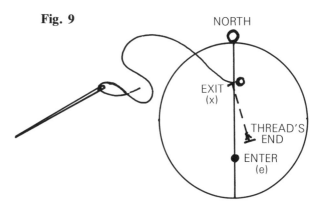

Fig. 9

Fig. 10

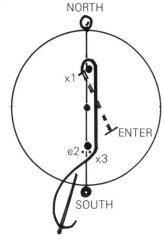

NORTH

x1

ENTER

e2 x3

SOUTH

Fig. 11

SOUTH

x3
e2

x1

NORTH

Fig. 12

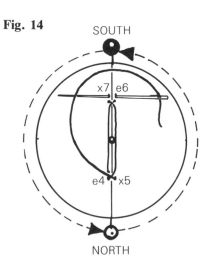

SOUTH

OBI

Hold the ball with your LEFT hand. With your RIGHT hand, carry the black thread around the TOP side of the 1/2 MARK PIN, along the RIGHT side of the OBI mark pin and around the bottom of the LOWER 1/2 MARK PIN. (Fig. 10)

TURN the ball so that the NORTH POLE is at the BOTTOM. Take above the pin a tiny stitch just under the mark line, catching 6 to 8 cover threads. (Fig. 11)

With the thumb of the LEFT hand, align the thread alongside the GOLD MARK LINE. (Fig. 12)

Fig. 13

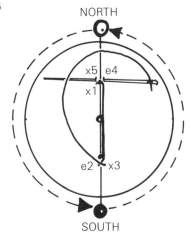

NORTH

x5 e4
x1

e2 x3

SOUTH

Fig. 14

SOUTH

x7 e6

e4 x5

NORTH

TURN the ball COUNTERCLOCKWISE so that the NORTH POLE is again on TOP. Take a tiny stitch under the mark line about 1/4 INCH ABOVE the first. (Fig. 13)

Align the thread with your left thumb and turn the ball COUNTERCLOCKWISE.
The SOUTH POLE is on TOP.
Take another stitch about 1/4 INCH ABOVE the first. (Fig. 14)

Fig. 15

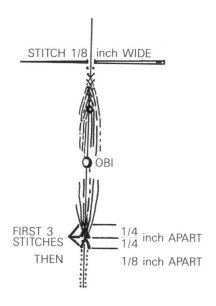

STITCH 1/8 inch WIDE

O OBI

FIRST 3 STITCHES — 1/4 1/4 inch APART

THEN — 1/8 inch APART

NOTE:
— Each time a new stitch is taken the thread should be adjusted and aligned next to the last thread by the thumb of the left hand and the thread should be pulled taut but not tight.
— Turn the ball each time you are ready to take a stitch so that the stitch is taken at the TOP
TURN the ball as you carry the thread to the opposite end. Carry the thread to the LEFT of the Obi Line pin each time.

For the rest of the pattern, each stitch should be spaced about 1/8 INCH ABOVE the last, with no more than 1/8 INCH BETWEEN the ENTRANCE and EXIT of the needle and the marking line in the center. (Fig. 15)

KEEP the SPACING UNIFORM each time a stitch is taken. As you continue you will find that your stitches and spacing will become more and more regular.

The BLACK (#310) SECTION should have 8 ROWS or 8 threads on each side of the gold mark line. It should measure approximately 3-1/8 INCHES or 8 centimeters in LENGTH and 5/8 INCH or 1.5 centimeters at its widest point in the center.

Lay each thread flat along the surface of the ball and move each so that it lines up alongside the one before. Be careful not to allow threads to overlap each other except at points where stitches are taken.

The shape of this pattern will look like the illustration in Figure 16.

Continue around the outside of the pattern until you have completed 8 ROWS of BLACK thread #310 on each side of the GOLD mark line. You should end up at the NORTH POLE END.

Fig. 16

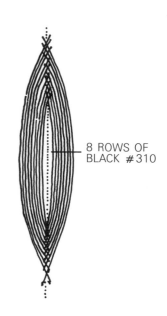

8 ROWS OF BLACK #310

ESCAPE the BLACK thread #310 by completing the final entrance and EXITING the needle DEEP beneath the ball's surface about 1-1/2 INCHES AWAY at an opposing angle. (Fig. 17)

With the LEFT hand, stretch the thread tightly out of the ball—with the RIGHT hand cut the thread where it exits the ball's surface. NO KNOT IS NECESSARY. (Fig. 18)

Cut a piece of YELLOW #973 that measures about 24 inches. Thread your needle. ENTER your needle so that it EXITS just OPPOSITE the end of the last black row. (Fig. 19)

Fig. 19

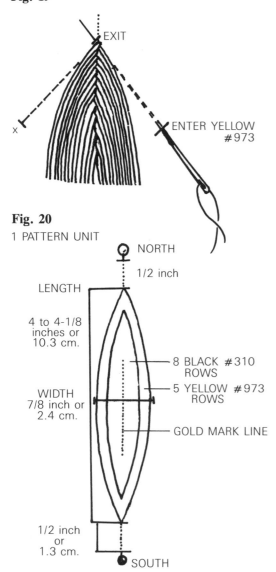

Fig. 20

1 PATTERN UNIT

Fig. 17

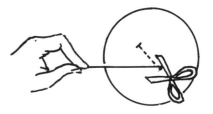

EXIT 1-1/2 inches AWAY

Fig. 18

Continue using this same stitch untill you have completed 5 YELLOW ROWS around the outside the 8 BLACK ROWS or 5 threads on each side. (Fig. 20)

ESCAPE the YELLOW thread #973.

The completed pattern unit of 8 BLACK ROWS and 5 YELLOW ROWS should measure approximately 4-1/8 INCHES or 10.3 centimeters in LENGTH and 7/8 INCH or 2.4 centimeters at its widest point.

The distance between the tip of the pattern and the NORTH and SOUTH POLE PINS should be about 1/2 INCH or 1.3 centimeters.

COMPLETE AN IDENTICAL PATTERN UNIT ON EACH OF THE SEVEN REMAINING DIVISION LINES.
Try to keep all 8 pattern units identical in size by marking the top and bottom ending points with a pin. Gauge your spacing as you work toward that end point.
This BASIC STITCH is the foundation of TEMARI embroidery. It is this basic stitch and the variety of different division possibilities that lead to an unlimited number of pattern combinations and designs.

The ball is complete.

BALL #2 "Friendship Chain"

This ball will use the basic pattern stitch to create interlocking squares.
A new stitch will be introduced which creates the starburst effect inside the center spaces.

MATERIALS:

One 3 inch ball, thread wrap in deep pink

DMC Pearl Cotton #5 in 3 colors:
  Pink #776
  Greens: Light Green #954
          Dark Green #943

Gold marking thread

Paper for tabs (typing or notebook paper)

Paper strip for marking

Fig. 1

<TOP VIEW>

NORTH

<SIDE VIEW>

NORTH

Fig. 2

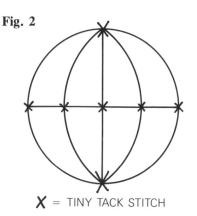

X = TINY TACK STITCH

MARK THE BALL into EIGHTHS with an OBI LINE. (Fig. 1)

DO NOT REMOVE PINS.

Use the GOLD THREAD TO MARK.

TACK the 8 INTERSECTIONS around the OBI LINE. (Fig. 2)
TACK the NORTH and SOUTH POLES.

DIVIDE EVERY OTHER marking line IN
HALF BETWEEN the OBI LINE and the
NORTH POLE and the OBI LINE and the
SOUTH POLE.
MARK each division with a PIN. (Fig. 3)

Fig. 3

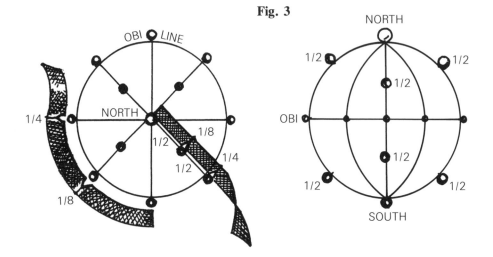

Fig. 4

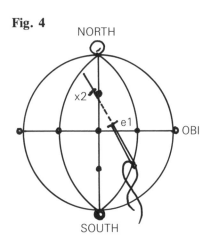

MEASURE about 30 inches of DARK
GREEN thread #943.
THREAD your NEEDLE.

TURN your BALL so that the NORTH POLE
is at the TOP and one DIVIDED MARKING
LINE FACES YOU. (Fig. 4)

ENTER (e1) your needle so that it EXITS (x2)
immediately to the LEFT of the NORTH
HALF MARK PIN.

PULL THREAD through CAREFULLY to
anchor.

TURN the BALL as you work so that each
stitch that is taken is at the top of the design.

(Fig. 5):
ENTER (e3) your needle immediately to the
RIGHT of the OBI LINE PIN. Take a TINY
stitch, catching the MARKING THREAD and
a few threads on the surface of the ball.
EXIT (x4) your needle immediately to the
LEFT of the OBI LINE PIN.

PULL the THREAD FIRMLY but
CAREFULLY.

Fig. 5

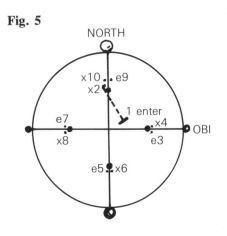

Fig. 6

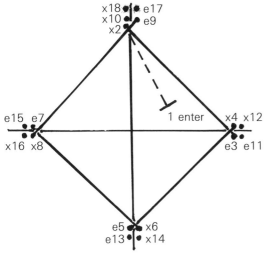

TURN the BALL a quarter turn, ready for the next stitch at the TOP.

ENTER (e5) your NEEDLE to the RIGHT of the HALF MARK PIN. Take a tiny stitch under the marking line. EXIT (x6) to the LEFT of the PIN.

TURN the BALL another quarter turn. Take the next stitch. (Fig. 6)

Fig. 7

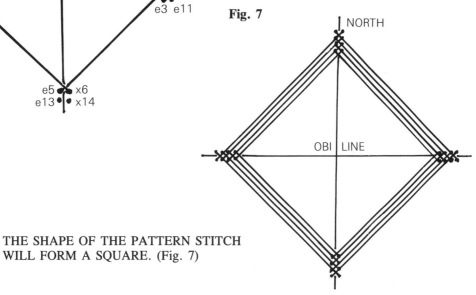

THE SHAPE OF THE PATTERN STITCH WILL FORM A SQUARE. (Fig. 7)

MAKE EACH STITCH VERY SMALL. CATCH THE MARKING THREAD PLUS 3–6 SURFACE THREADS.

KEEP EACH STITCH IMMEDIATELY ABOVE THE LAST. DO NOT LEAVE SPACE IN BETWEEN.

COMPLETE 4 ROWS using DARK GREEN #943.

ESCAPE the DARK GREEN thread #943. (Fig. 8)

Fig. 8

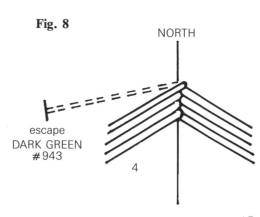

MEASURE about 36 inches of PINK #776.
THREAD your NEEDLE.

ENTER the PINK thread #776 so that it
EXITS immediately to the LEFT of the LAST
GREEN. (Fig. 9)

Fig. 9   **Fig. 10**

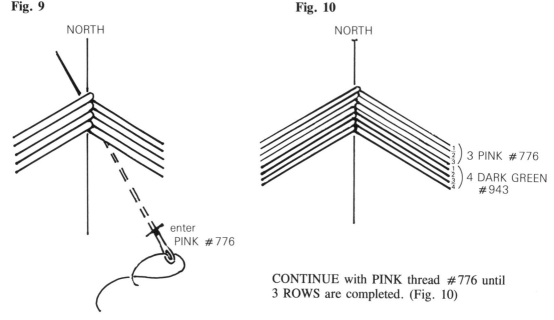

CONTINUE with PINK thread #776 until
3 ROWS are completed. (Fig. 10)

BEGIN AND END EACH COLOR ON THE
NORTH POLE CORNER.

If you run out of thread, don't worry.
Just make your escape, MARK YOUR
PLACE, and continue to completion.

SAVE the LONGER SCRAPS of THREAD,
you can use them when you run short.

Fig. 11

(Fig. 11)
THE COMPLETED SQUARE PATTERN:

4 rows	DARK GREEN #943	4 DARK GREEN #943
3	PINK #776	3 PINK #776
3	LIGHT GREEN #954	3 LIGHT GREEN #954
5	PINK #776	5 PINK #776
2	LIGHT GREEN #954	2 LIGHT GREEN #954
3	PINK #776	3 PINK #776
1	DARK GREEN #943	1 DARK GREEN #943
21 rows	TOTAL	21 ROWS TOTAL

46

Fig. 12

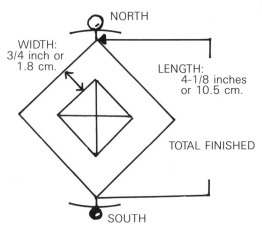

THE FIRST COMPLETE SQUARE MEASUREMENTS (Fig. 12)

NORTH

WIDTH: 3/4 inch or 1.8 cm.

LENGTH: 4-1/8 inches or 10.5 cm.

TOTAL FINISHED

SOUTH

Fig. 13

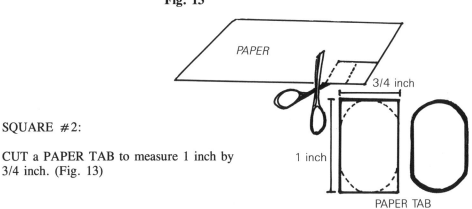

PAPER

3/4 inch

1 inch

PAPER TAB

SQUARE #2:

CUT a PAPER TAB to measure 1 inch by 3/4 inch. (Fig. 13)

Fig. 14

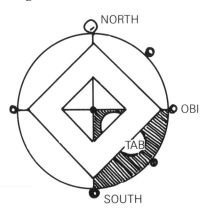

NORTH

OBI

TAB

SOUTH

Fig. 15

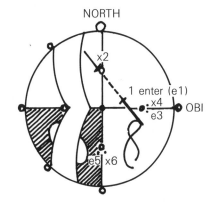

NORTH

x2

1 enter (e1)
x4
e3
OBI

e5 x6

HOLD the BALL so that the NORTH POLE is at the TOP and your completed SQUARE FACES YOU. (Fig. 14)
SLIDE the TAB UNDER the threads of the LOWER RIGHT QUARTER.

TURN the BALL to the NEXT DIVIDED MARKING LINE on the RIGHT. (Fig. 15)

ENTER (e1) and begin the next square in the very same way as you started square #1.

Fig. 16

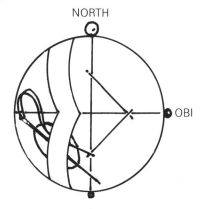

NORTH

OBI

Fig. 17

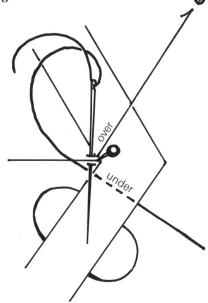

over

under

When you reach the TAB, PUSH the NEEDLE THROUGH EYE-END FIRST. (Fig. 16)

TAKE the FIRST STITCH in the very SAME WAY as before but move it in CLOSE TO THE CORNER of the completed square. (Fig. 17)

REPEAT the identical COLOR PATTERN that was used for square #1.
Complete square #2 in the SAME way as square #1, using the TAB to create the interlock. (Fig. 18)

SQUARE #3:

REMOVE the TAB from square #2 or cut another.

TURN the BALL to the NEXT DIVIDED MARKING LINE on the RIGHT.

Again SLIDE the TAB UNDER the threads of the LOWER RIGHT QUARTER of square #2. (Fig. 19)

Fig. 18

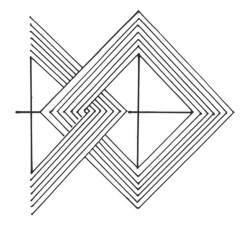

COMPLETE square #3 using the TAB to create the interlock.

Fig. 19

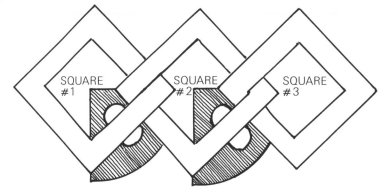

SQUARE #1

SQUARE #2

SQUARE #3

SQUARE #4:

CUT 2 TABS.

With NORTH POLE at the TOP, turn the ball
so the LAST REMAINING DIVIDED
MARKING LINE FACES YOU. (Fig. 20)

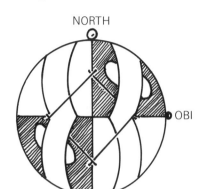

Fig. 20

Slide ONE TAB under the threads in the
UPPER RIGHT QUARTER of the ball.

Slide the SECOND TAB under the threads of
the LOWER LEFT QUARTER of the ball.

BEGIN the final square at the NORTH POLE
CORNER and complete the pattern with 2
INTERLOCKS.

REMOVE the paper TABS and PINS.

Fig. 21

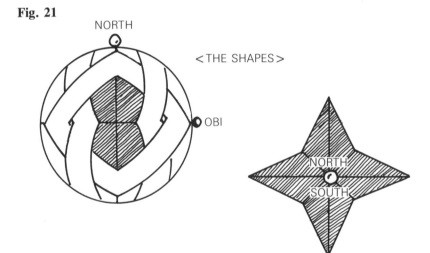

< THE SHAPES >

THE STARBURSTS:

A simple Starburst stitch fills in the spaces in
the center of each square and the star shapes
at the North and South Poles. (Fig. 21)

USE the GOLD marking thread.

With your NEEDLE, CENTER the GOLD
MARKING THREADS if they have slipped
out of place.

MEASURE about 24 inches of GOLD thread.
THREAD your NEEDLE and KNOT one end.

ENTER (e1) thread and PULL FIRMLY so
that the KNOT sinks UNDER the SURFACE.
(Fig. 22)

Fig. 22

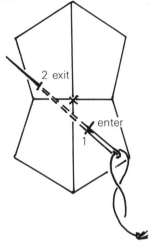

FOLLOW the NUMBERS.

CROSS THROUGH the CENTER intersection
EACH TIME. (Fig. 23)

Fig. 23

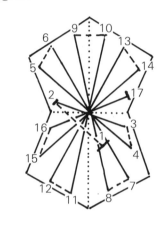

Fig. 24

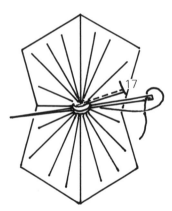

After #17, EXIT the NEEDLE just on the
LEFT side of CENTER. (Fig. 24)

Take 2—3 TACK stitches of the CENTER to
CATCH ALL of the THREADS.

ESCAPE the GOLD thread.

TACK the threads in the CENTER with a
cross-stitch. (Fig. 25)

The ball is complete.

Fig. 25

< TOP and BOTTOM >

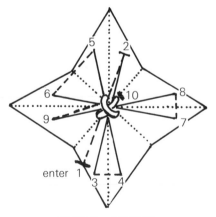

TACK the CENTER

BALL #3 "Merry-go-round"

On this ball the basic stitch will be used in an alternating zig-zag pattern which will create diamond shapes around the ball.
An Obi or belt will secure the stitches.

MATERIALS:

One 3 inch ball, thread wrap in Christmas green

DMC Pearl Cotton #5 in 4 colors:
  Light Green #954
  Orange #946
  Peachs: Light Peach #353
          Dark Peach #352

Gold or Silver marking thread

Paper strip for marking

Fig. 1

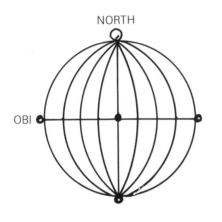

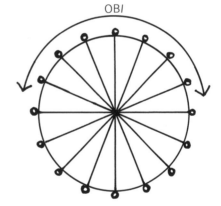

MARK THE BALL into SIXTEENTHS with an OBI LINE. (Fig. 1)

Refer to "Marking the Ball" (page 32) for help.

MARK the ball using the GOLD or SILVER marking thread.

TACK the NORTH and SOUTH POLES (Fig. 2)
TACK each of the 16 INTERSECTIONS around the Obi Line.

Fig. 2

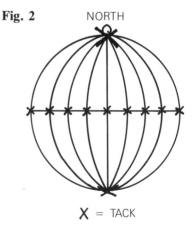

X = TACK

51

Fig. 3

NORTH

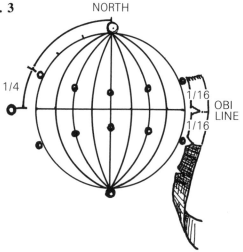

1/4

1/16

1/16

OBI
LINE

Fig. 4

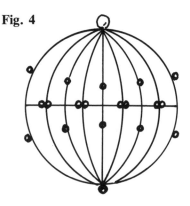

Fig. 5

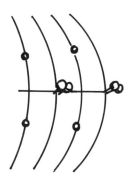

By marking the ball into sixteenths, your paper measure has been notched into sixteenths.

On EVERY OTHER LINE around the ball, MEASURE AND MARK with a pin:
    1/16 ABOVE the OBI LINE
and, 1/16 BELOW the OBI LINE (Fig. 3)

NOTE: To help check your measurement, 1/16 of the paper strip = 1/4 the distance from the NORTH POLE to the OBI LINE.

On each of the IN—BETWEEN LINES, insert 2 PINS at the OBI LINE INTERSECTION. (Fig. 4) These are the KEEPER PINS.

Insert the KEEPER PINS so that they stick out about 1/4 INCH from the ball's surface and so that they stand ONE ON EACH SIDE of the MARKING LINE. Place each pair of pins as CLOSE TOGETHER as possible. (Fig. 5)

SAVE YOUR PAPER MEASURE.

THE ZIG-ZAG PATTERN:
(Fig. 6)

Fig. 6

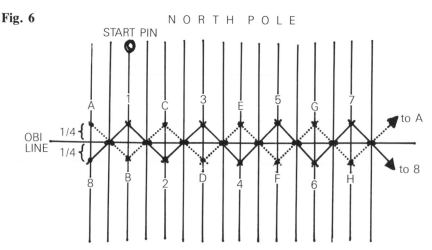

Insert a different colored PIN up near the North Pole on one of the lines with sixteenth marks on it. This will mark your STARTING PLACE (#1 PIN).

To follow the zig-zag pattern, first look ONLY at the NUMBERS in Figure 6. Start with the number 1. FOLLOW the NUMBERS 1 through 8 around the ball in a ZIG-ZAG until you return to the number 1.

Begin with your GOLD or SILVER thread.

(You can MEASURE the amount you will need simply by wrapping the thread in the zig-zag pattern around the sixteenth mark pins.)

MEASURE enough thread for 2 zig-zags around the ball plus about 8 inches.

THREAD your NEEDLE.

KNOT one thread end.

Fig. 7

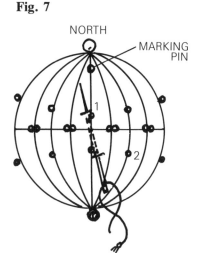

Fig. 8

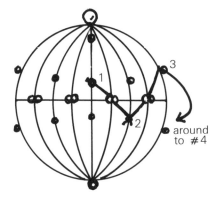

ENTER the needle so that it EXITS just to the LEFT of the #1 pin. Pull the thread through carefully so that the knot disappears below the surface of the ball. (Fig. 7)

FEED the THREAD THROUGH the middle of the two KEEPER PINS on the NEXT LINE to the RIGHT. (The keeper pins keep the threads in line).

CARRY the thread to the #2. (Fig. 8) Take a small STITCH around the OUTSIDE of (BELOW) the #2 pin.

FEED the thread through the NEXT two KEEPER PINS on the way to #3.

Take a small STITCH around the OUTSIDE of (ABOVE) the #3 PIN.

Go on to #4.

YOU DO NOT NEED TO TURN THE BALL UPSIDE DOWN EACH TIME YOU TAKE A STITCH.

CONTINUE to follow the numbers around the ball until you return to the #1 PIN.

Again at the #1 pin, take a STITCH just
ABOVE the first stitch. (Fig. 9)

ALIGN the second thread OUTSIDE of the
first thread, FLAT AGAINST THE BALL.

At the keeper pins the SECOND thread will
CROSS OVER the FIRST thread.

At the #2 PIN, take a stitch just BELOW the
first stitch. Align the thread around the
OUTSIDE of the first thread.

Carry the thread through the keeper pins to
#3. Take a stitch just above the last.
Align the thread.

KEEP THE THREAD LINES CLOSE
TOGETHER to achieve a double-wide line
of gold or silver.

CONTINUE the zig-zag until 2 ROWS are
completed and you have RETURNED to the
#1. ESCAPE the thread at the #1.

MEASURE the metallic thread for 2 more
zig-zags around the ball.

Now look only at the LETTERS on the
diagram.

ENTER the needle so that it EXITS to the
LEFT of the LETTER A pin (2 lines to the
left of the #1 pin, above the #8 pin).
(Fig. 10)

NOW FOLLOW THE LETTERS.

COMPLETE 2 ROWS in silver or gold using
the LETTERED PINS. (Fig. 11)
ESCAPE the thread.

Fig. 9

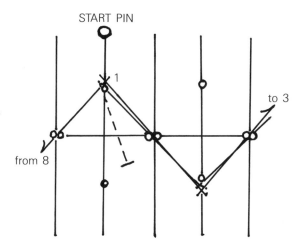

Fig. 10

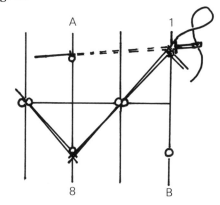

Fig. 11

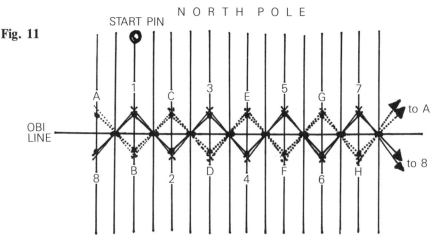

54

Fig. 12

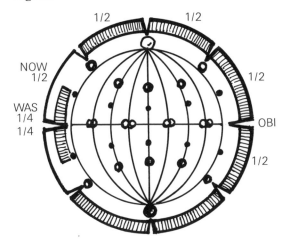

REMOVE the sixteenth mark PINS from all 8 lines around the ball.

On the SAME 8 LINES,
MEASURE and MARK with a PIN:
      1/2 way between the NORTH POLE
                   and the OBI LINE,
      1/2 way between the SOUTH POLE
                   and the OBI LINE. (Fig. 12)

LEAVE THE KEEPER PINS WHERE THEY ARE.

Again using the GOLD or SILVER and the NEW PIN MARKS, MEASURE enough thread for 2 ZIG-ZAGS around the ball plus about 8 INCHES.

Thread your needle.

Fig. 13

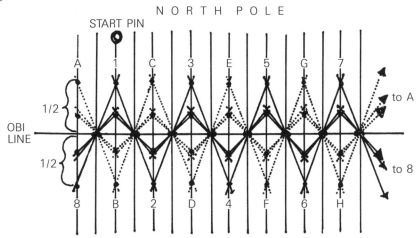

COMPLETE 1 ROW of silver using the NUMBERS, COMPLETE 1 ROW using the LETTERS. (Fig. 13)

ESCAPE the thread. REMOVE the PINS.

Fig. 14

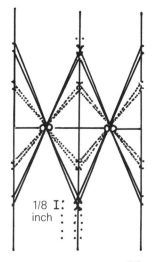

Now as you use the colored threads, SPACE all of your STITCHES about 1/8 INCH APART, TOP and BOTTOM. (Fig. 14)

Fig. 15

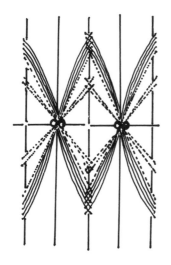

Beginning with the DARK PEACH #352:
Do 2 ROWS using the NUMBERS
    2 ROWS   LETTERS
    2 ROWS   NUMBERS
    2 ROWS   LETTERS
for a TOTAL of 4 rows TOP and 4 rows BOTTOM. (Fig. 15)

IMPORTANT NOTE: Alternating the threads, one or two rows at a time, helps to stack them more securely between the keeper pins.

With the ORANGE #946:
Do 1 ROW   NUMBERS
   1 ROW   LETTERS

With the LIGHT PEACH #353:
Do 3 ROWS NUMBERS
   3 ROWS LETTERS

With the GREEN #954:
Do 3 ROWS NUMBERS
   3 ROWS LETTERS

Fig. 16

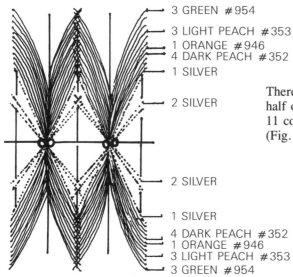

3 GREEN #954
3 LIGHT PEACH #353
1 ORANGE #946
4 DARK PEACH #352
1 SILVER

2 SILVER

There should be 11 colored threads on the top half of the diamond and, identically, 11 colored threads on the bottom half. (Fig. 16)

2 SILVER

1 SILVER
4 DARK PEACH #352
1 ORANGE #946
3 LIGHT PEACH #353
3 GREEN #954

Fig. 17

THE OBI STITCH:

The Obi Stitch will secure each cluster of threads that is held by the keeper pins. (Fig. 17)

To begin, WORK RIGHT NEXT TO THE OBI LINE, TOP AND BOTTOM.

ALTERNATE your ROWS from one side of the Obi Line to the other EACH TIME.

MEASURE the ORANGE thread #946 by
taking 2 WRAPS around the ball plus about
10 INCHES. (Fig. 18)

Thread your needle.

Fig. 18

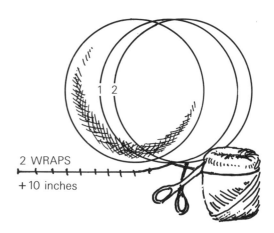

2 WRAPS
+10 inches

Fig. 19

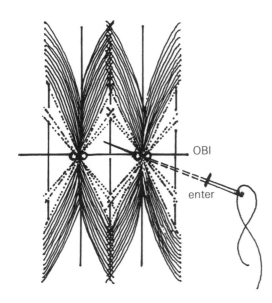

OBI

enter

ENTER the needle so that it EXITS just to the
LEFT of one cluster of threads and its keeper
pins, and JUST ABOVE THE OBI LINE.
(Fig. 19)

Fig. 20

Take a stitch UNDER the cluster, catching
ALL the threads and a few background
threads.
Pull the stitch FIRMLY around the cluster and
adjust its position to lay JUST ABOVE the
Obi Line. (Fig. 20)

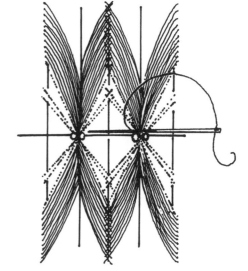

Carry the thread alongside the Obi Line to the next cluster of threads to the LEFT.
Take a stitch. (Fig. 21)

Continue to the next cluster on the LEFT and take a stitch, LINING UP the ORANGE THREAD #946 carefully just ABOVE the Obi Line.

Continue around the Obi Line until all 8 clusters have a stitch to secure them.

Fig. 21

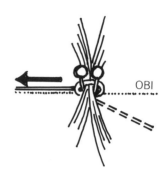

OBI

Fig. 22

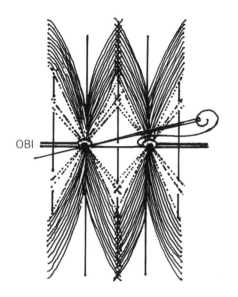

OBI

At the final cluster, EXIT the thread so that the next row begins just BELOW the OBI Line Mark. (Fig. 22)

Continue around the ball making a row BELOW the Obi Line.
Slide the two stitches CLOSE TOGETHER on each cluster.

Make a TOTAL of 3 ROWS of ORANGE #946 ABOVE the Obi Line and 3 ROWS BELOW. (Fig. 23)

Allow the Obi Mark Line to show in the middle.

Using the LIGHT PEACH thread #353, do 1 ROW ABOVE and 1 ROW BELOW to outline the Obi.

The ball is complete.

Fig. 23

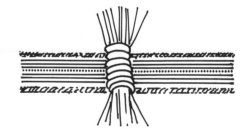

BALL #4 "Triplets"

On this ball, interlocking squares with alternating layers of threads provide a design of three diamonds which form the three points of equilateral triangles. The order in which the threads are applied is the key to this design.

This design will use the space around the OUTSIDE of each square rather than the space within the square.

MATERIALS:

One 3 inch ball, thread wrap in light yellow

DMC Pearl Cotton #5 in 5 colors:
 Black #310
 White #5
 Light Green #954
 Yellow #444
 Orange #741

Gold marking thread

Paper strip for marking

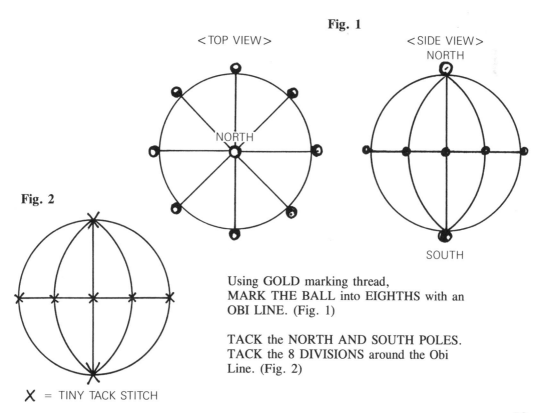

Fig. 1

<TOP VIEW>

NORTH

<SIDE VIEW>
NORTH

SOUTH

Fig. 2

Using GOLD marking thread, MARK THE BALL into EIGHTHS with an OBI LINE. (Fig. 1)

TACK the NORTH AND SOUTH POLES. TACK the 8 DIVISIONS around the Obi Line. (Fig. 2)

X = TINY TACK STITCH

Fig. 3

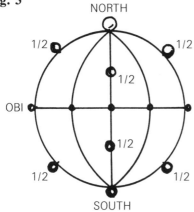

DIVIDE EVERY OTHER division line in HALF ABOVE and BELOW the Obi Line as in Ball #2. (Fig. 3)

With your GOLD marking thread, connect the pin measurements to form 4 SQUARES AROUND the Obi Line. (Fig. 4)

To MARK the 4 squares around the Obi, USE the BASIC STITCH. Take each STITCH around the OUTSIDE of each PIN.

Fig. 4

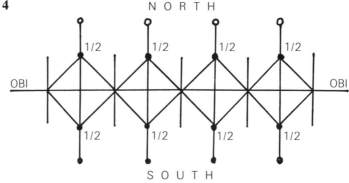

Fig. 5

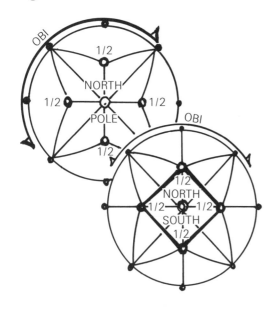

CONNECT the 4 HALF-MARK PINS at the TOP and BOTTOM (around the North and South Poles) to MAKE 2 MORE SQUARES. (Fig. 5)

There will now be a TOTAL of 6 SQUARES marked on the ball in gold thread. (Fig. 6)

Fig. 6

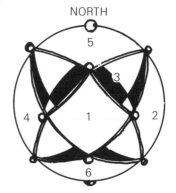

Fig. 7

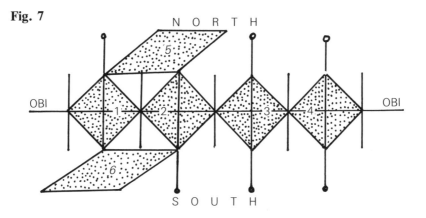

Next we will decide on a NUMERICAL PATTERN to work by. This pattern will be REPEATED in the SAME ORDER EACH TIME until the ball is complete. (Fig. 7)

I recommend doing squares 1 and 2, then 3 and 4, around the Obi; then the North Pole square (5), then the South Pole square (6).

MARK each square with a numbered paper tab and a pin. (Fig. 8)
MARK your STARTING PLACE in each square with your "NUMBER PIN" so that you will start in the same place each time.

Fig. 8

You can CONNECT 2 of the OBI LINE SQUARES such as 1 and 2, and 3 and 4 (Fig. 9), CARRYING your THREAD from one to the other.
The North and South Pole squares are difficult to connect. It is easier to do them individually, at least in the beginning.

Fig. 9

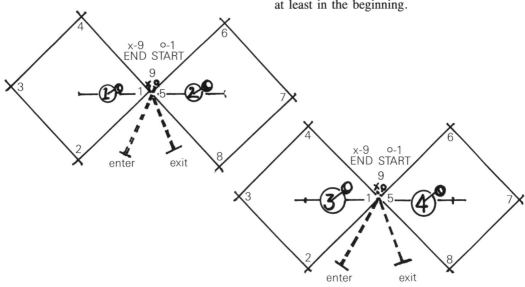

THREAD your NEEDLE with BLACK thread #310.

Fig. 10

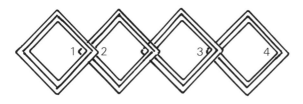

Do 3 ROWS of BLACK #310 AROUND the
OUTSIDE MARKING THREAD of the #1
SQUARE. (Fig. 10)

Do 3 ROWS of BLACK #310 AROUND the
OUTSIDE MARKING THREAD of the #2
SQUARE.

3 ROWS around #3 square.

3 ROWS around #4 square.

Fig. 11

5 and 6

3 ROWS around the NORTH POLE square
(#5). (Fig. 11)
3 ROWS around the SOUTH POLE square
(#6).

THREAD your NEEDLE with WHITE thread
#5.

Using the SAME ORDER of squares that you
used previously,
BEGIN AGAIN AT SQUARE #1.

Do 3 ROWS of WHITE #5 around the
OUTSIDE of the BLACK on each of the 6
SQUARES. (Fig. 12)

Fig. 12

AGAIN using the SAME ORDER of squares,
THREAD your NEEDLE with the GREEN
thread #954:

Do 2 ROWS of GREEN #954
around the outside of each of the 6
SQUARES.

Do 2 MORE ROWS of GREEN
#954 around each of the 6
SQUARES, for a TOTAL of 4
GREEN ROWS around each square.

Fig. 13

Your thread will form a layered pattern at
each end of each diamond shape. (Fig. 13)

The pattern developing will look like this:
(Fig. 14)

Fig. 14

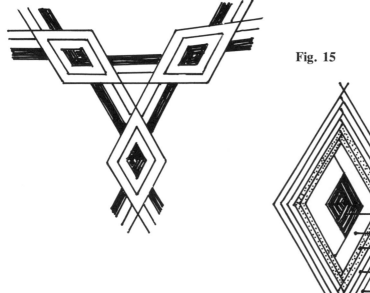

Fig. 15

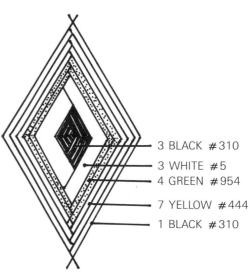

3 BLACK #310
3 WHITE #5
4 GREEN #954
7 YELLOW #444
1 BLACK #310

With the YELLOW thread #444:
  Do 2 ROWS around each square
  Do 2 ROWS AGAIN—each square
  Do 3 ROWS MORE—each square
for a TOTAL of 7 ROWS of YELLOW
#444. (Fig. 15)

With the BLACK thread #310:
  Do 1 ROW around each square.

When this is completed you may TACK the
LAST BLACK OUTLINE ROW into place
with black sewing thread.

Fig. 16

To finish the ball, use the ORANGE thread
#741 to stitch a SOLID SQUARE into the
CENTER of each of the 6 original squares.
(Fig. 16)

TO STITCH THE SQUARE:

MEASURE about 18 inches of ORANGE thread #741.

TURN the ball so that the NORTH POLE is at the TOP and one EMPTY CENTER of a PATTERN FACES YOU. (Fig. 17.1)

ENTER the needle so that it EXITS immediately to the LEFT of an OBI LINE intersection with its VERTICAL LINE in the center.

PULL THREAD through CAREFULLY to anchor it.

BEGIN the CENTER STITCH by FOLLOWING the NUMBERS in Figures 17.2 through 17.8.

Fig. 17.1

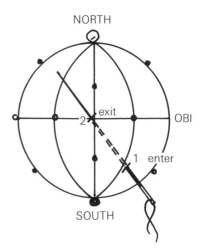

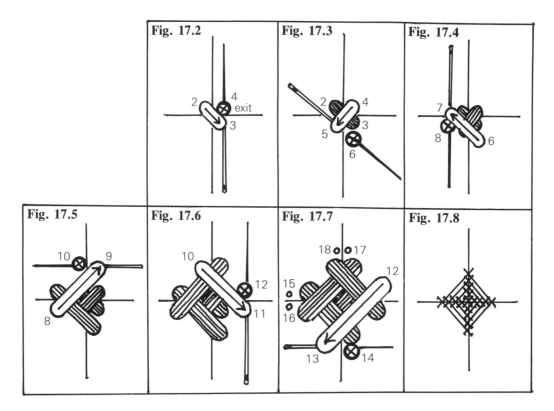

Fig. 18

Remember:
with each stitch you take—cross OVER 2 adjacent marking lines and UNDER 1. (Fig. 18)

The ball is complete.

BALL #5 "Columbine"

This ball will use six equal measurements around the Obi and will introduce the wrapping technique of ball design. After measuring the ball into sixths, longitudinal lines will be applied by wrapping over the ball's surface. The stitched pattern and Obi will be applied on top of these wrapped lines.

The stitched pattern will incorporate the ordered application of threads as on Ball #4.

MATERIALS:

One 3 inch ball, thread wrap in black

One small spool of bright royal blue sewing thread

DMC Pearl Cotton #5 in 6 colors:
    White #5
    Blues: Light Blue #747
           Medium Blue #996
           Dark Blue #995
    Yellow-Orange #742
    Orange #946

Gold marking thread

Paper strip for marking

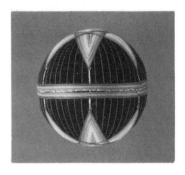

Fig. 1

<TOP VIEW> <SIDE VIEW>

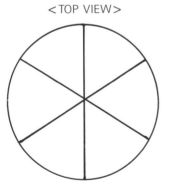

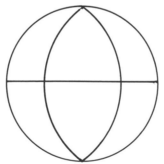

Fig. 2

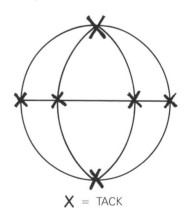

X = TACK

To measure the ball into SIXTHS with an OBI line, find the NORTH and SOUTH POLES. DIVIDE the NORTH to SOUTH measurement in HALF to locate the OBI. Measure around the Obi with your paper strip divided into SIXTHS. (Find THIRDS first then divide thirds in HALF) (Fig. 1)
Use the GOLD THREAD to mark the sixths.

TACK the NORTH and SOUTH POLES. TACK each of the SIX INTERSECTIONS around the Obi Line. (Fig. 2)

Fig. 3

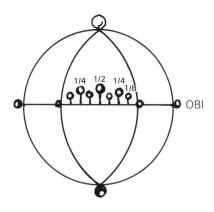

Hold the ball so that the OBI LINE FACES YOU.

Using one section (the space between 2 marking lines), take your pins and divide and mark the Obi Line of that section first in half, then into fourths, then into eighths. (Fig. 3) (Your eye will provide you with an accurate enough measurement, a paper measure is not necessary).

Fig. 4

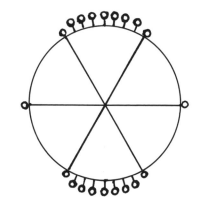

TURN the ball so that the EXACT OPPOSITE section faces you.

Again DIVIDE that OPPOSITE SECTION in HALF, then FOURTHS and EIGHTHS with your pins. (Fig. 4)

THREAD your NEEDLE with the BLUE SEWING THREAD. DO NOT CUT THE THREAD FROM THE SPOOL. (Fig. 5)

It will not be necessary to cut the thread until this entire process is complete.

Fig. 5

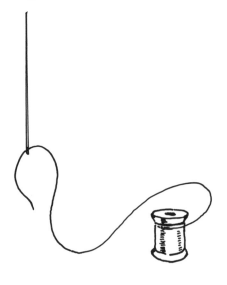

ENTER your NEEDLE at the NORTH POLE PIN so that it EXITS about 1-1/2 inches BELOW. (Fig. 6)

Fig. 6

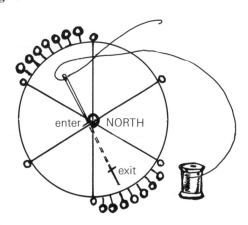

Pull the needle and thread through the ball's surface.
REMOVE the NEEDLE from the THREAD.

KNOT the THREAD'S END. (Fig. 7)

PULL the KNOT back through firmly until it DISAPPEARS UNDER the ball's SURFACE. (Fig. 8)

You now have an entire spool of thread attached to your ball and NO NEEDLE on the thread.

Fig. 7

Fig. 8

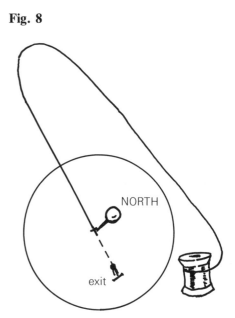

HOLD the SPOOL of thread in one hand and the ball in the other.

WRAP a LINE of thread over the ball starting at the NORTH POLE, continuing along side of (to the left of) the first "Mark Pin," to the SOUTH POLE. (Fig. 9)

CONTINUE back up the other side to the EXACT OPPOSITE "Mark Pin," and back to the North Pole.

Fig. 9

WRAP 1 MORE THREAD LINE immediately over the first line so there are 2 THREADS by each pin.

GO ON to the SECOND "Mark Pin."
WRAP a LINE around the ball.
WRAP A SECOND on top of the first.
Go on to the third "Mark Pin."

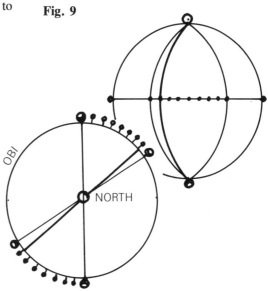

Fig. 10

MARK PINS

2 THREADS

NORTH/SOUTH PINS

WRAP 2 THREAD LINES for EACH "MARK PIN."

BE CONSISTENT:

WRAP always on the SAME SIDE of EACH MARK PIN.

WRAP always on the SAME SIDE of the NORTH and SOUTH POLE PINS as the lines move around the circle. (Fig. 10)

If you do this your measurements and lines will be more accurate and it will be easier to tack the North and South Pole threads at the end.

Fig. 11

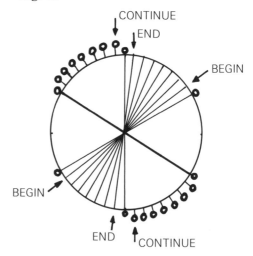

CONTINUE

END

BEGIN

BEGIN

END   CONTINUE

Continue to wrap 2 lines for each pin until the first 2 sections are completed.

Then move the "Mark Pins" to divide the 2 sections next to the sides you ended on. (Fig. 11)

This way you can continue right on around the ball.

Fig. 12

SKIP OVER the GOLD MARKING LINE and BEGIN again at the FIRST "MARK PIN."

COMPLETE the next 2 OPPOSITE SECTIONS. (Fig. 12)

MOVE your PINS to the REMAINING 2 OPPOSITE SECTIONS and COMPLETE their wrapping.

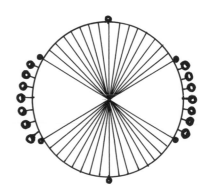

Fig. 13

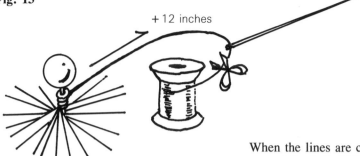

+ 12 inches

When the lines are completed all the way around the ball, END at the NORTH POLE where you began, SECURE your THREAD temporarily by winding it 3—4 times around the North Pole pin. (Fig. 13)

Pull off about 12 INCHES OF EXTRA THREAD from the spool and CUT the SPOOL from the BALL.

THREAD your NEEDLE with the 12 INCHES.
UNWIND your THREAD from the North Pole pin.

Fig. 14

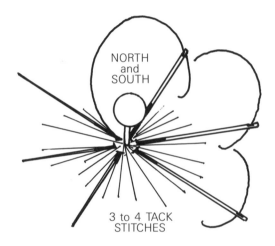

NORTH and SOUTH

3 to 4 TACK STITCHES

With SEVERAL TINY CROSS STITCHES, TACK the NORTH POLE THREADS at the CENTER.
Be sure to catch ALL threads BEFORE REMOVING the North Pole pin. (Fig. 14)

TACK the South Pole threads.

YOU DO NOT NEED TO TACK ALL THE THREADS THAT ARE WRAPPED AROUND THE OBI.

Fig. 15

REMOVE the PINS.

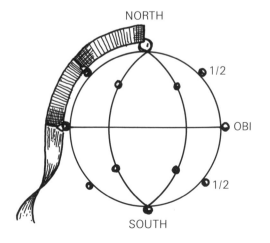

NORTH

1/2

OBI

1/2

SOUTH

Again take your PAPER MEASURE:

DIVIDE each GOLD MARKING LINE in HALF BETWEEN the NORTH POLE and the OBI LINE and the SOUTH POLE and the OBI LINE and MARK each division with a PIN. (Fig. 15)

Again, as in Ball #4, the threads will be applied in a numerical order. The SAME order will be repeated each time.

Thread your needle with the YELLOW-ORANGE thread #742.

For this pattern the BASIC STITCH used in Ball #1 will be applied, but the position of the stitch will change after each stitch is taken.

ENTER your needle so that it EXITS to the LEFT of a HALF MARK PIN. (Fig. 16) Pull the thread through.

Fig. 16

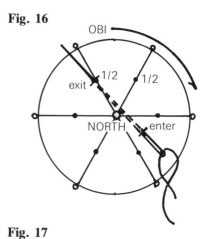

TURN the ball so that the OPPOSITE HALF MARK PIN is at the TOP. Take another stitch ABOVE the OPPOSITE HALF MARK PIN.

Return to the first side to complete the stitch. ENTER the needle to the RIGHT of the pin to complete the first stitch BUT so that it EXITS on the LEFT of the NEXT GOLD MARKING LINE to the LEFT. (Fig. 17)

Fig. 17

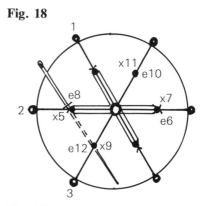

Take a second stitch on the second Marking Line. Continue on to the third Marking Line. Take a stitch over the first two. (Fig. 18)

Fig. 18

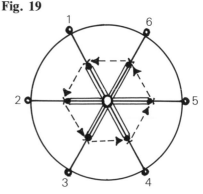

Continue to #4, take a stitch.

Go to #5, take a stitch.

Go to #6, take a stitch, for a total of 2 YELLOW-ORANGE (#742) ROWS with the centers built one on top of the other around the circle. (Fig. 19)

Fig. 19

REPEAT in exactly the same way at the SOUTH POLE END.

EACH TIME you take a STITCH, MOVE
ONE LINE to the LEFT.

Fig. 20

1/8 inch

Now SPACE your STITCHES about 1/8
INCH APART down each Marking Line.
(Fig. 20)

THREAD your NEEDLE with the WHITE
thread #5. BEGIN with #1, DO 3 ROWS of
WHITE #5, ONE at a TIME, around the
OUTSIDE of the 2 rows of yellow-orange
#742 on the NORTH and SOUTH Pole ends.
(Fig. 21)

Fig. 21

— 2 YELLOW-
ORANGE #742

With the LIGHT BLUE thread #747:
    Do 3 ROWS (one at a time) around each
    of the white rows, North and South.

With the MEDIUM BLUE thread #996:
    Do 3 ROWS (one at a time) around each
    of the light blue rows, North and South.

Fig. 22

— 3 WHITE #5

With the DARK BLUE thread #995:
    Do 1 ROW
    around the medium blue rows, North
    and South. (Fig. 22)

The Star pattern is complete.

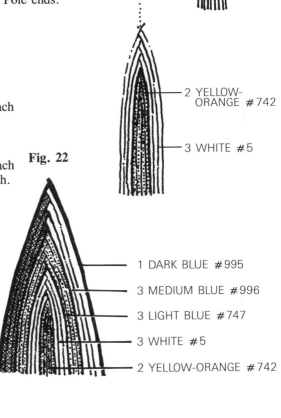

1 DARK BLUE #995

3 MEDIUM BLUE #996

3 LIGHT BLUE #747

3 WHITE #5

2 YELLOW-ORANGE #742

Fig. 23

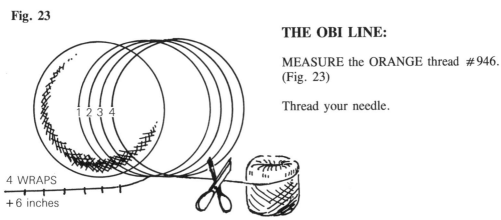

1 2 3 4

4 WRAPS

+6 inches

THE OBI LINE:

MEASURE the ORANGE thread #946.
(Fig. 23)

Thread your needle.

Fig. 24

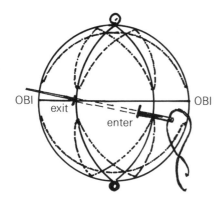

Fig. 25

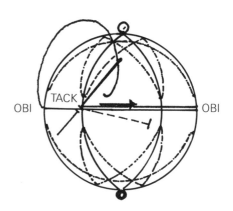

ENTER your NEEDLE so that it EXITS at the INTERSECTION OF THE OBI LINE and ONE GOLD DIVISION LINE. (Fig. 24)

PULL the THREAD through until the END DISAPPEARS under the ball's surface.

WRAP the THREAD in the OPPOSING DIRECTION back around the ball at the Obi Line.
ALIGN the ORANGE thread #946 next to the GOLD OBI MARK LINE. (Fig. 25)

When the first orange wrap around the Obi Line is complete, take a tiny TACK stitch NEXT to the Obi Line.

WRAP the ORANGE thread #946 a SECOND TIME around the Obi, aligning it closely ABOVE the first orange line.

When you are back at the beginning, ESCAPE the ORANGE #946 so that it EXITS just BELOW the OBI LINE. (Fig. 26)

WRAP one line around next to the Obi Line, TACK it.
WRAP ONE MORE LINE around BELOW the first, for a TOTAL of 4 ORANGE LINES, 2 ABOVE the OBI MARK LINE and 2 BELOW.

ESCAPE the ORANGE #946.

USE a DIFFERENT STARTING PLACE around the Obi EACH TIME you start a new color.

Fig. 26

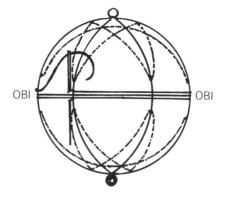

72

Fig. 27

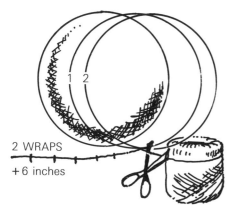

2 WRAPS

+6 inches

MEASURE the YELLOW-ORANGE thread #742. (Fig. 27)

Thread your needle with the YELLOW-ORANGE thread #742.

Do 1 yellow-orange (#742) row ABOVE the orange.

Do 1 yellow-orange (#742) row BELOW the orange.

ESCAPE the yellow-orange #742.

MEASURE the MEDIUM BLUE thread #996. (Fig. 27)

Do 1 row of medium blue #996 ABOVE and BELOW the yellow-orange #742.

Fig. 28

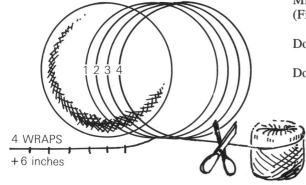

4 WRAPS

+6 inches

MEASURE the DARK BLUE thread #995. (Fig. 28)

Do 2 rows ABOVE, TACK EACH row.

Do 2 rows BELOW, TACK EACH.

Fig. 29

O   B   I

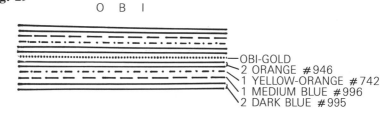

OBI-GOLD
2 ORANGE #946
1 YELLOW-ORANGE #742
1 MEDIUM BLUE #996
2 DARK BLUE #995

There should now be a TOTAL of 12 thread lines around the Obi. (Fig. 29)

The ball is complete.

BALL #6 "Wishing Papers"

On this ball a layered wrapping technique will be used over a mark of six equal divisions around the Obi. A stitched Obi will secure the wrapped threads at every sixth division.

MATERIALS:

One 3 inch ball, thread wrap in light chartreuse (greenish-yellow)

DMC Pearl Cotton #5 in 10 colors:
 Blues: Light Blue #598, Medium Blue #597
  Dark Blue #806
 Greens: Light Green #472, Medium Green #471
  Dark Green #470
 Purples: Light Purple #211, Medium Purple #209
  Dark Purple #208, Darkest Purple #550 (Obi)

Gold marking thread

Paper strip for marking

Fig. 1

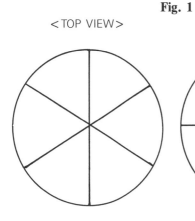

\<TOP VIEW\>   \<SIDE VIEW\>

Fig. 2

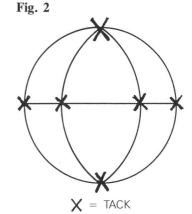

X = TACK

Fig. 3

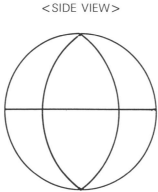

NORTH

1/2

OBI

1/2

SOUTH

MEASURE THE BALL into SIXTHS with an OBI LINE. (Fig. 1)

TACK the North and South Poles.
TACK each of the 6 INTERSECTIONS around the Obi. (Fig. 2)

With your PAPER STRIP, divide EACH of the 6 MARK LINES in HALF between the North Pole and the Obi Line and between the South Pole and the Obi Line. (Fig. 3)

74

Insert 2 "KEEPER PINS" at each of the 6 intersections AROUND the OBI. (Fig. 4)

MEASURE 2 wraps plus 6 inches of GOLD THREAD. (Fig. 5)

Thread your needle. KNOT the thread's end.

Hold the ball with the NORTH POLE at the TOP.

ENTER your needle so that it EXITS at ONE of the Obi Line intersections. (Fig. 6)
Pull the gold thread firmly so that the KNOT DISAPPEARS beneath the ball's surface.

Fig. 4

OBI

Fig. 5

1 2

2 WRAPS
+6 inches

Fig. 6

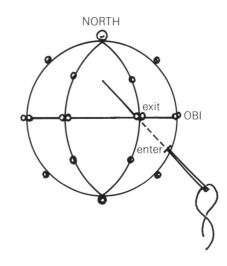

NORTH

exit OBI

enter

WRAP the first line of GOLD thread so that it goes DIAGONALLY around the ball on the LEFT side of the North pole. (Fig. 7)

It should lie just BELOW each 1/2 MARK PIN, through the KEEPER PINS on the exact OPPOSITE SIDE of the Obi, just ABOVE the 1/2 MARK PINS on the SOUTH Pole side, and back to the starting place.

Fig. 7

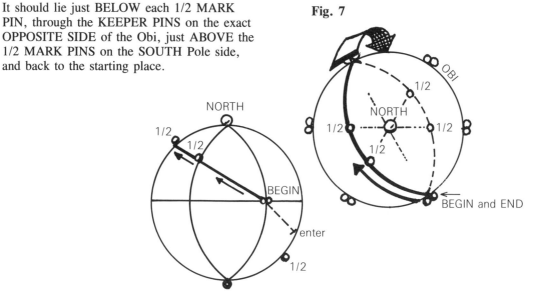

NORTH

1/2
1/2

BEGIN

enter

1/2

OBI

1/2

NORTH

1/2   1/2

1/2

BEGIN and END

Fig. 8

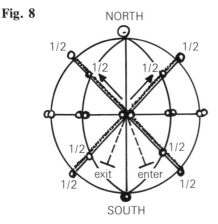

Back at the starting place, take a tiny TACK stitch, then WRAP the gold thread DIAGONALLY toward the RIGHT in the same manner. (Fig. 8)
ESCAPE the GOLD thread.

Thread your needle with the DARK BLUE thread #806.

Hold the ball with the NORTH POLE at the TOP.

ENTER the needle through the OBI INTERSECTION so that it EXITS ABOVE the OBI LINE. (Fig. 9)

Pull the needle and thread end through.
REMOVE the NEEDLE from the thread.
Pull the thread END back through carefully until it DISAPPEARS under the ball's surface. (Fig. 10)

You now have your whole spool of DARK BLUE thread #806 attached to the ball with NO NEEDLE.

Fig. 9

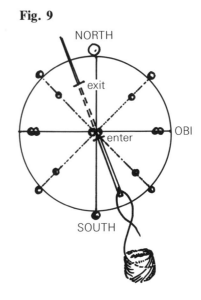

Fig. 10

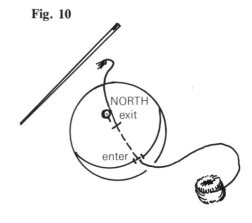

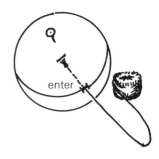

Fig. 11

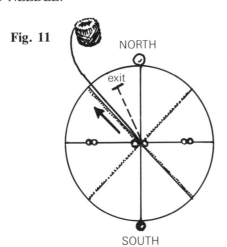

Again starting toward the LEFT 1/2 Mark Pins, begin to WRAP the DARK BLUE thread #806 onto the ball so that it lies immediately ALONGSIDE the diagonal GOLD thread. (Fig. 11)

76

Fig. 12

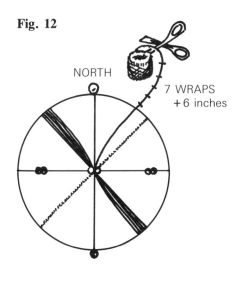

NORTH

7 WRAPS
+ 6 inches

Wrap the DARK BLUE #806 around the ball in this direction 7 TIMES. (Fig. 12)
As you progress, each line should lie NEARER to the NORTH AND SOUTH POLES.

Use the THUMB of the LEFT HAND to ALIGN each thread next to the last and hold it in place. (Fig. 13)

Fig. 13

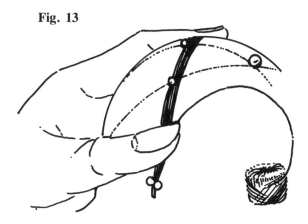

When 7 lines are completed and you are back where you started, cut the thread from the ball allowing about 6 inches extra.
Thread your needle with the extra.

(You don't have enough hands, eh?)
Stick the needle into the ball so that you don't have to hold it, then put the thread through the eye.

ESCAPE the DARK BLUE #806 toward the SOUTH Pole. (Fig. 14)

Fig. 14

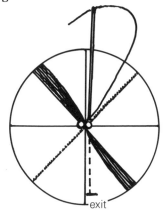

exit

Thread your needle with the SAME DARK BLUE #806.

WRAP 7 MORE times on the DIAGONAL toward the RIGHT. (Fig. 15)

Cut your thread with 6 extra inches, thread your needle and escape the DARK BLUE #806 toward the SOUTH POLE.

Fig. 15

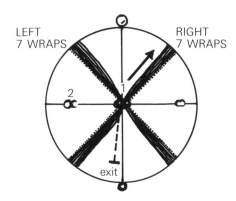

LEFT
7 WRAPS

RIGHT
7 WRAPS

2

1

exit

Move to the NEXT OBI INTERSECTION to the LEFT. (Fig. 16)

MEASURE 2 wraps plus 6 inches of GOLD thread.

Do a GOLD DIAGONAL line toward the LEFT, TACK, do a GOLD DIAGONAL line toward the RIGHT.

ESCAPE the gold.

Thread your needle with the DARK PURPLE #208, not the darkest #550, that's for the Obi.

Start toward the LEFT in the very same way as with the blue. ENTER the needle and thread so that it EXITS at the OBI. REMOVE the NEEDLE, DISAPPEAR the END and WRAP the thread 7 TIMES around, aligning each thread carefully next to the last.

Back at the beginning, cut the thread from the ball allowing 6 inches extra, thread the needle and ESCAPE the DARK PURPLE #208.

Do 7 WRAPS of DARK PURPLE #208 on a diagonal to the RIGHT.

Move to the NEXT Obi INTERSECTION to the LEFT. (Fig. 17)
 Do 1 Diagonal gold line LEFT
  1 Diagonal gold line RIGHT
  7 wraps of DARK GREEN #470 to the LEFT
  7 wraps of DARK GREEN #470 to the RIGHT

Move to the NEXT Obi intersection on the LEFT (BLUE):
 Do 1 gold LEFT
  1 gold RIGHT
  7 DARK BLUE #806 to the LEFT
  7 DARK BLUE #806 to the RIGHT
  (Fig. 18)

Move to the NEXT Obi intersection on the LEFT (PURPLE):
 Do 1 gold LEFT
  1 gold RIGHT
  7 DARK PURPLE #208 to the LEFT
  7 DARK PURPLE #208 to the RIGHT

Move ONE intersection to the LEFT (GREEN):
 Do 1 gold LEFT
  1 gold RIGHT
  7 DARK GREEN #470 to the LEFT
  7 DARK GREEN #470 to the RIGHT

Fig. 16

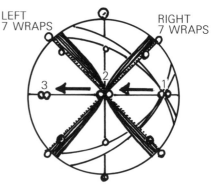

Fig. 17

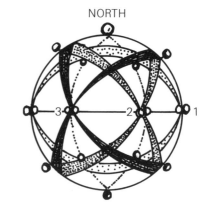

Fig. 18

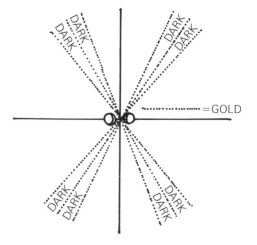

Fig. 19

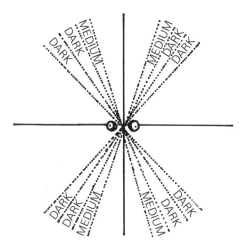

Fig. 20

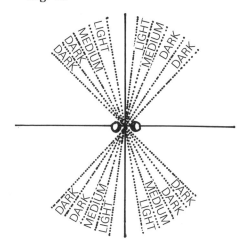

Fig. 21

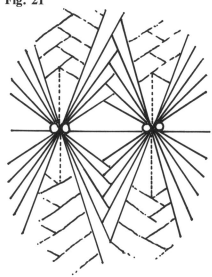

Now USE the MEDIUM SHADES of the 3 colors.
(Fig. 19)
Move ONE intersection to the LEFT (BLUE):
    Do 1 gold LEFT
        1 gold RIGHT
        7 MEDIUM BLUE #597 to the LEFT
        7 MEDIUM BLUE #597 to the RIGHT

Move ONE intersection to the LEFT (PURPLE):
    Do 1 gold LEFT
        1 gold RIGHT
        7 MEDIUM PURPLE #209 to the LEFT
        7 MEDIUM PURPLE #209 to the RIGHT

On to the LEFT (GREEN):
    Do 1 gold LEFT
        1 gold RIGHT
        7 MEDIUM GREEN #471 to the LEFT
        7 MEDIUM GREEN #471 to the RIGHT

NOTE: BE SURE THE KEEPER PINS ARE
       CLOSE TOGETHER.
       Stacks of threads between the Keeper
       Pins will line up neater and stay in
       place if you keep the Keeper Pins
       close together.

Now USE the LIGHT SHADES of the 3 colors.
(Fig. 20)
On to the Blue:
    Do 1 gold LEFT
        1 gold RIGHT
        7 LIGHT BLUE #598 to the LEFT
        7 LIGHT BLUE #598 to the RIGHT
        1 GOLD LEFT
        1 GOLD RIGHT to finish the CENTER

On to the Purple:
    Do 1 gold LEFT
        1 gold RIGHT
        7 LIGHT PURPLE #211 to the LEFT
        7 LIGHT PURPLE #211 to the RIGHT
        1 gold LEFT
        1 gold RIGHT

On to the Green:
    Do 1 gold LEFT
        1 gold RIGHT
        7 LIGHT GREEN #472 to the LEFT
        7 LIGHT GREEN #472 to the RIGHT
        1 gold LEFT
        1 gold RIGHT

Layers of threads will look as if they are
interwoven across the surface of the ball.
(Fig. 21)

Fig. 22

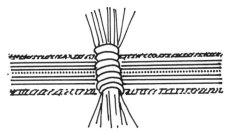

Fig. 23

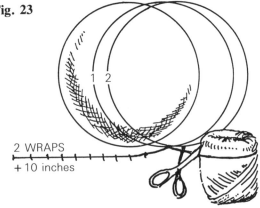

2 WRAPS
+ 10 inches

THE OBI LINE:

As on Ball #3, the Obi will "back stitch" over each cluster of threads and anchor it into place. (Fig. 22)

MEASURE 2 WRAPS plus 10 INCHES of GOLD thread. (Fig.23)

Thread your needle. Knot the end.

ENTER the needle so that it EXITS to the LEFT of one thread CLUSTER just ABOVE the Obi Line. (Fig. 24)

Pull the thread through so the knot disappears.

Take a stitch BACKWARD over the thread cluster, just ABOVE the Obi Line. Pull the thread firmly around the cluster so that it is securely anchored. (Fig. 25)

Fig. 24

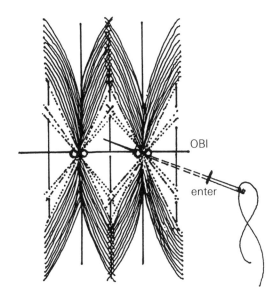

OBI

enter

Move to the NEXT cluster to the LEFT. ENTER the needle UNDER the cluster. Take a BACK STITCH around the cluster. ALIGN the gold thread so that it lies just ABOVE the Obi Line. (Fig. 26)

Fig. 25

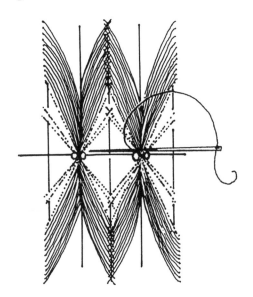

Fig. 26

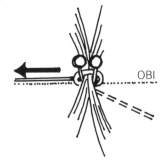

OBI

Fig. 27

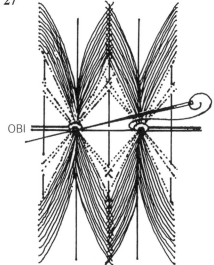

OBI

Continue around the ball taking a stitch at each cluster.

Back at the BEGINNING, EXIT the needle to just BELOW the Obi Line. (Fig. 27)

Continue around the ball taking another stitch at each cluster, just BELOW the Obi Line.

MEASURE 5 WRAPS of the DARKEST PURPLE #550. (Fig. 28)

Fig. 28

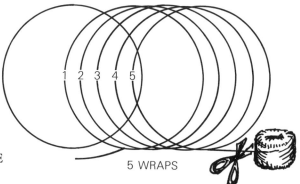

1 2 3 4 5

5 WRAPS

ENTER the needle so that it EXITS ABOVE the Obi Line. (Fig. 29)

Do 2 DARKEST PURPLE (#550) ROWS ABOVE the Obi Line.

Do 2 DARKEST PURPLE (#550) ROWS BELOW the Obi Line.

Measure more thread.

Do 2 MORE purple lines ABOVE.

Do 2 MORE BELOW.

Do 1 GOLD LINE ABOVE,
   1 GOLD LINE BELOW.

Fig. 29

1 GOLD
4 PURPLE #550
1 GOLD
OBI
1 GOLD
4 PURPLE #550
1 GOLD

The ball is complete.

BALL #7 "Spinning Top"

This ball uses six equal divisions around the Obi Line. Two three-pointed star designs are stitched in numerical order, one on top of the other, to form a central hexagon. The Obi is first wrapped onto the ball then cross-stitched over to complete the pattern.

MATERIALS:

One 3 inch ball, thread wrap in bright purple

DMC Pearl Cotton #5 in 4 colors:
    Yellow-Orange #742
    Red #606
    Dark Green #943
    Dark Blue #995

Silver metallic marking thread

Paper strip

Fig. 1

<TOP VIEW>

<SIDE VIEW>

Fig. 2

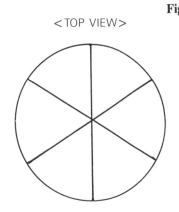

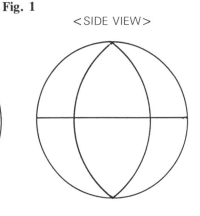

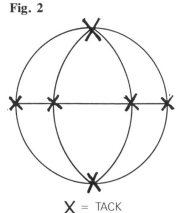

X = TACK

Fig. 3

MEASURE THE BALL into SIX equal divisions with an OBI LINE. Use the SILVER thread to mark. (Fig. 1)

TACK the NORTH and SOUTH POLE threads.
TACK the SIX intersections around the Obi Line. (Fig. 2)

With your PAPER MEASURE divide EVERY OTHER marking line in HALF between the NORTH POLE and the OBI LINE.
At the SOUTH POLE end, divide the SAME 3 lines in HALF between the SOUTH POLE and the OBI LINE. (Fig. 3)

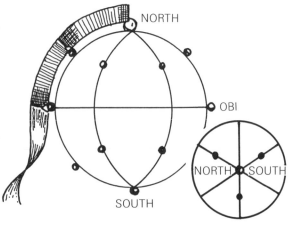

82

Thread your needle with about 36 inches (1 yard) of YELLOW-ORANGE thread #742.

Begin this design by stitching a hexagon around the North Pole pin. (Fig. 4)

Mark your STARTING PLACE with a PIN.

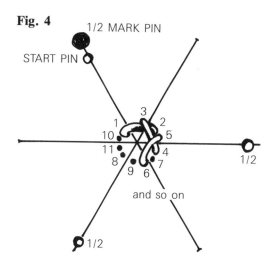

Fig. 4

1/2 MARK PIN

START PIN

1/2

1/2

and so on

Fig. 5

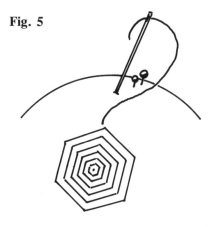

Complete 6 ROWS around the North Pole to make the central hexagon.

END where you BEGAN. (Fig. 5)

This ending should be on a line that has a 1/2 MARK PIN.

Now that you have completed the hexagon, continue with the same thread into the three-pointed pattern. Follow the numbers in each diagram.

Fig. 6

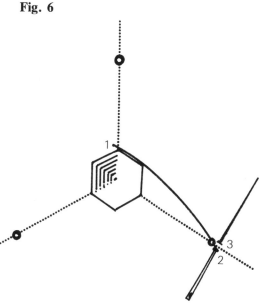

Fig. 7

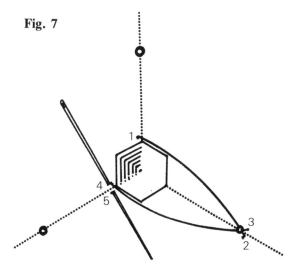

Carry the thread alongside the hexagon and beyond it to the next 1/2 MARK PIN to the RIGHT. (Fig. 6)

TAKE A STITCH around the OUTSIDE of the 1/2 MARK PIN.

Carry the thread back in to the hexagon. (Fig. 7)

Take a stitch VERY CLOSE to the hexagon.

Fig. 8

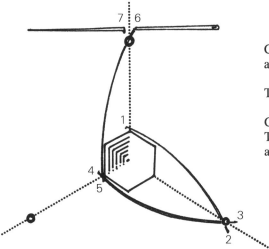

Carry the thread to the next 1/2 MARK PIN around CLOCKWISE. (Fig. 8)

Take a stitch OUTSIDE the 1/2 MARK PIN.

Carry the thread back to the hexagon. (Fig. 9) Take a stitch close to the hexagon's point at 8 and 9.

Fig. 9

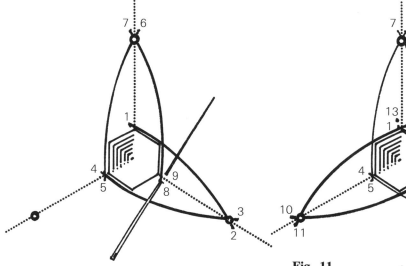

Fig. 10

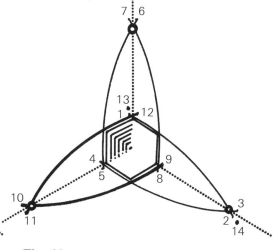

Carry the thread to the REMAINING 1/2 MARK PIN. (Fig. 10) Take a stitch outside the 1/2 mark pin at 10 and 11.

Continue to 12 and 13 to complete the firist row.

Follow the numerical MAP in Figure 11 to continue the pattern.

Fig. 11

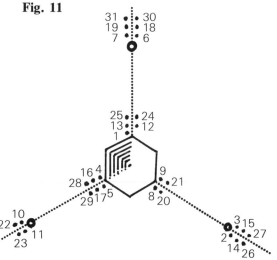

Fig. 12

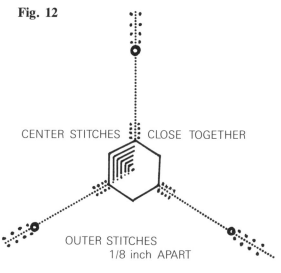

CENTER STITCHES :: CLOSE TOGETHER

OUTER STITCHES
1/8 inch APART

Fig. 13

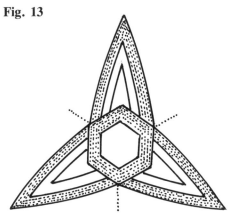

NOTE: Stitches that are made in the CENTER, NEXT TO the HEXAGON, should be kept CLOSE TOGETHER.
Stitches at the OUTSIDE POINTS should be spaced 1/8 INCH APART. (Fig. 12)

Complete 4 ROWS in YELLOW-ORANGE #742.

END on the SAME MARK LINE where you BEGAN.

Thread your needle with about 1-1/2 yards of RED thread #606. This will NOT be enough to complete the orange section. Go as far as you can with this amount, escape and replenish the thread to complete the orange.

Begin on the SAME mark line where you ended the YELLOW-ORANGE #742.

Use the SAME NUMERICAL ORDER.

Complete 7 ROWS of RED #606 around the OUTSIDE of the yellow-orange #742. (Fig. 13)

The completed orange points should extend to about 1/2 inch above the Obi Line if you are spacing your stitches 1/8 inch apart.

Fig. 14

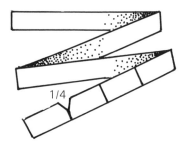

1/4

Fig. 15

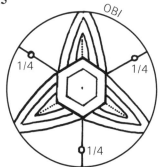

Take your PAPER MEASURE and fold it into the original FOURTHS that you used to locate the Obi Line. MARK one fold with a pencil mark.
Take that ONE FOURTH and DIVIDE it into FOURTHS. (Fig. 14)
Notch one of those fourths with your scissors.

Use this 1/4 measurement for the 3 REMAINING mark lines.

Measure UP from the Obi Line this 1/4 measurement on EACH of the 3 remaining mark lines. (Fig. 15)
MARK each measurement with a PIN.

Thread your needle with the GREEN thread #943, a long length.

The GREEN #943 and BLUE #995 threads will use the remaining 3 mark lines and will form a layer on top of the Yellow-orange #742 and Red #606.

ENTER your needle so that it EXITS on a HEXAGON POINT IN BETWEEN 2 LONG POINTS. (Fig. 16)

Use the SAME PATTERN with the NEW 1/4 MEASUREMENT on these 3 lines. (Fig. 17)

Remember your SPACING:
IN CLOSE to the CENTER HEXAGON,
OUT 1/8 INCH APART toward the OBI.

Complete 6 ROWS of GREEN #943 and
        1 ROW of BLUE #995. (Fig. 18)

REPEAT this ENTIRE PATTERN IDENTICALLY on the SOUTH POLE END.

Fig. 16

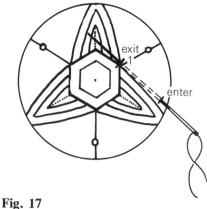

Fig. 17

Fig. 18

— 7 RED #606
— 4 YELLOW-ORANGE #742

— 6 GREEN #943
— 1 BLUE #995

THE OBI LINE:

This ball will use a flat wrapped Obi in alternating bands of yellow-orange #742 and silver. A cross-stitch pattern will be applied on top.

REMEMBER: Work from the CENTER Obi MARK LINE to the OUTSIDE. MEASURE your threads.

Figure 19 shows the WRAPPED PORTION of the OBI. A total of 15 lines.

COMPLETE the WRAPPED PORTION.

Fig. 19

3 SILVER
3 YELLOW-ORANGE #742
OBI and 2 SILVER
3 YELLOW-ORANGE #742
3 SILVER

THE CROSS STITCH PATTERN:

Place a PIN in the CENTER of each
TRIANGLE formed by the purple space
in between the points. (Fig. 20)

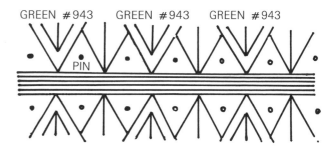

Fig. 20

GREEN #943   GREEN #943   GREEN #943

PIN

MEASURE 2 WRAPS of SILVER
thread.

Stitch a ZIG-ZAG line going from the
LOWER SIDE of the Obi, up to the
PIN, back to the next LOWER side
of the Obi. (Fig. 21)

Fig. 21

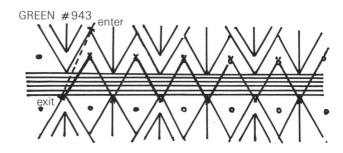

GREEN #943   enter

exit

Fig. 22

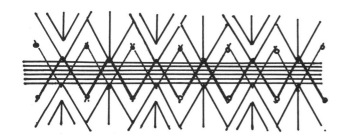

TURN THE BALL UPSIDE-DOWN.
Stitch the SAME ZIG-ZAG line in
SILVER so that a DIAMOND
PATTERN is formed over the Obi
Line. (Fig. 22)

Fig. 23

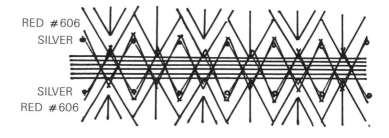

RED #606
SILVER

SILVER
RED #606

With RED thread #606 stitch another LINE
BELOW the silver on each side. (Fig. 23)

The ball is complete.

BALL #8 "Garland of Ribbons"

This ball displays a broad and ornate Obi as the dominant part of its design. Interlocking lines create the braided ribbon pattern around the Obi.

This is a design in which the number of division lines around the Obi can be changed to create a variety of different Obi effects on future balls, experiment with different numbers. Try alternating the beginning points of the different thread groups.

MATERIALS:

One 3 inch ball, thread wrap in Light Purple
    (same color as DMC #554)

DMC Pearl Cotton #5 in 7 colors:
    Purples: Light Purple #554
              Medium Purple #552
              Dark Purple #550
    Magenta #601
    Dark Green #943
    Light Blue #598
    White: #5

Silver marking thread

Fine Silver thread (sewing machine weight)

Tissue paper or rice paper (not Kleenex)

Paper strip for marking

Fig. 1

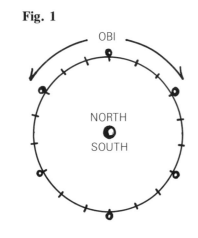

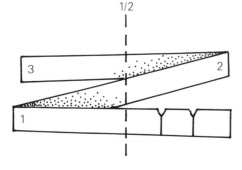

MEASURE the BALL into EIGHTEENTHS:

DIVIDE your PAPER STRIP into THIRDS, then SIXTHS. MARK the SIXTHS with a PENCIL.

DIVIDE the FIRST or LAST sixth measurement at either end of the paper into THIRDS.

With PINS, DIVIDE the OBI into SIXTHS, then DIVIDE EACH SIXTH division into THIRDS. (Fig. 1)

Use the HEAVIER weight SILVER marking thread for the 18 divisions and the Obi Line. Refer to Ball #3 for review.

Fig. 2

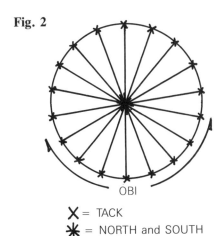

X = TACK

✳ = NORTH and SOUTH

TACK the NORTH and SOUTH POLE threads.
TACK the 18 divisions around the Obi Line. (Fig. 2)

Fig. 4

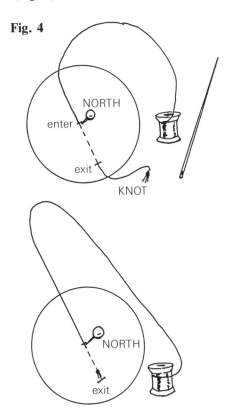

Remember:
ENTER the thread with the NEEDLE THROUGH the NORTH POLE.

REMOVE the NEEDLE, KNOT the thread's END. Pull the thread back through until the KNOT DISAPPEARS beneath the ball's surface. (Fig. 4)

Fig. 3

NORTH/SOUTH PINS

With the LIGHTWEIGHT SILVER sewing thread, WRAP every THIRD section of the eighteen so that SIX sections are covered with the lightweight silver thread. (Fig. 3)
ALIGN the THREADS.
WRAP always on the SAME SIDE of the NORTH and SOUTH POLE PINS as the lines move around the circle.

Fig. 5

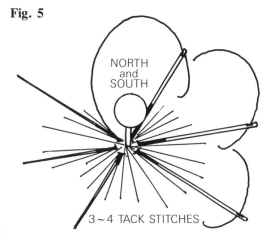

TACK all of the WRAPPED SILVER threads securely at the NORTH and SOUTH POLES. (Fig. 5)

89

Fig. 6

11-1/2 inches approximately

1-1/2 inches

FOLD

Fig. 7

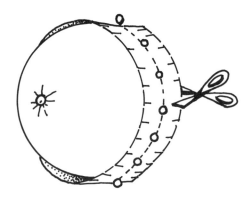

TO MARK THE WIDE OBI:

Carefully cut a strip of tissue paper 1-1/2 inches wide and long enough to wrap once around the Obi Line and overlap 1/2 to 3/4 inch at the end. (Fig. 6)

FOLD the strip accurately in HALF LENGTH-WISE.

PIN the tissue strip around the OBI LINE of the ball. MATCH the FOLD CAREFULLY around the OBI MARK LINE. This will center the paper strip accurately above and below. (Fig. 7)

With your SCISSORS, SNIP around BOTH SIDES of the PAPER. Make snips about 1/2 inch long, about 3/4 inch apart.

Thread your needle with your LIGHT PURPLE WRAP THREAD.

BASTE the paper strip to the ball with a row of stitches about 1/8 inch from the paper's edge on BOTH EDGES.

Use the snips to help you smooth the paper to fit the surface of the ball. (Fig. 8)

REMOVE the PINS from around the Obi.

Fig. 8

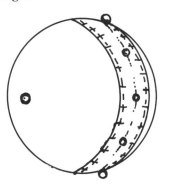

Fig. 9

NORTH

START

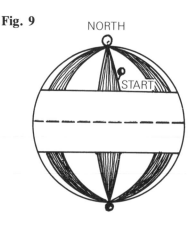

Turn your ball so that the North Pole is at the TOP. Place a PIN on the RIGHT SIDE EDGE of the SILVER section that faces you. This will be your START PIN. (Fig. 9)

Fig. 10

Thread your needle with a long length of WHITE THREAD #5.

ENTER your needle through the tissue of the Obi area so that it EXITS AT THE START PIN LINE AND JUST ABOVE THE PAPER STRIP. (Fig. 10)

Pull the thread through until the end disappears beneath the paper.

TURN the BALL so that the NEXT SILVER SECTION to the RIGHT faces you. (Fig. 11)

Take a stitch on the RIGHT SIDE EDGE just BELOW the PAPER.

Fig. 11

When you take a stitch, CATCH ONLY 3—4 threads on the ball's surface. Make the stitch VERY TINY.

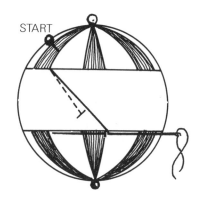

Fig. 12

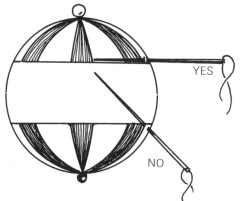

YES

NO

Try to keep each stitch HORIZONTAL along the paper's edges. DO NOT TAKE THE STITCH AT AN ANGLE. (Fig. 12)

Fig. 13

At the NEXT SILVER SECTION on the RIGHT, take a tiny stitch on the RIGHT SIDE EDGE ABOVE the paper strip. (Fig. 13)

Fig. 14

Turn the ball again to the next section on the RIGHT. Take a stitch BELOW.

CONTINUE AROUND THE BALL with this ZIG-ZAG line until you return to the START PIN. (Fig. 14)

CLOSE the zig-zag line by taking a tiny stitch. (Fig. 15)

Fig. 15

ALIGN the SECOND THREAD to the LEFT of the FIRST.

Continue moving around the ball to the RIGHT.

Take the next stitch at each point JUST TO THE LEFT of the first stitch. (Fig. 16)

Fig. 16

REMEMBER:

    Keep your stitches very TINY above and below the paper.

    Catch only 3—4 surface threads each time you take a stitch.

    Keep your stitches VERY CLOSE TOGETHER at the top and bottom. It takes a lot of threads to cover that fat belly under the Obi.

Fig. 17

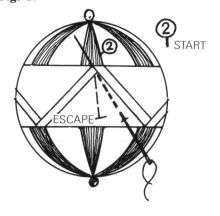

Do 5 ROWS of WHITE #5 in a zig-zag around the ball. END where you BEGAN. EXIT the thread into the Obi area through the tissue and ESCAPE. (Fig. 17)

Thread your needle with the LIGHT PURPLE thread #554.

ENTER your needle so that it EXITS immediately to the LEFT of the 5 WHITE (#5) ROWS.

Fig. 18

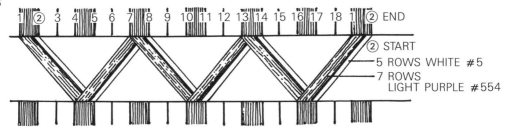

Continue in the very same way.

Do 7 ROWS of LIGHT PURPLE #554 next to the 5 WHITE (#5) ROWS. (Fig. 18) The 5 WHITE (#5) ROWS and 7 LIGHT PURPLE (#554) ROWS should fill in the space between the two edges of the silver section. (Fig. 19)

Fig. 19

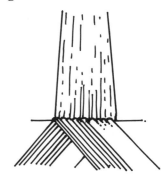

Fig. 20

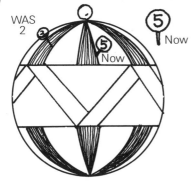

MOVE your START PIN over to the RIGHT side EDGE of the NEXT SILVER SECTION to the RIGHT. (Fig. 20)

Thread your needle with the GREEN thread #943.

ENTER your needle so that it EXITS just ABOVE the paper on the NEW START PIN LINE. (Fig.21)

Fig. 21

Do 3 ROWS of GREEN #943 in a zig-zag around the ball ON TOP of the Light Purple #554 and White #5 lines.

Do 9 ROWS of MEDIUM PURPLE #552 starting immediately to the LEFT of the 3 GREEN (#943) rows. (Fig. 22)

Fig. 22

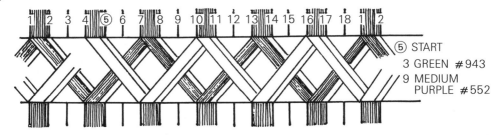

The 3 GREEN (#943) and 9 MEDIUM PURPLE (#552) rows will fill the space between the edges of those silver sections around the ball. (Fig. 23)

MOVE your START PIN to the LEFT edge of the silver section (one marking line to the left). (Fig. 24)

Your START PIN corresponds to the 4 in Figure 25.

Fig. 23

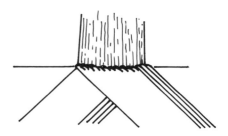

Thread your needle with SILVER MARKING THREAD, enough for 2 ROWS around the ball.

ENTER your needle so that it EXITS immediately LEFT of the LAST row of MEDIUM PURPLE #552.

Do 2 ROWS of SILVER.

Do 9 ROWS of MAGENTA #601 to the LEFT of the silver.

Do 2 MORE ROWS of SILVER to cover the spaces between the marking lines. (Fig. 25)

MOVE the START PIN to the LEFT ONE MARK LINE (to the 3 in Figure 25).

Fig. 24

Fig. 25

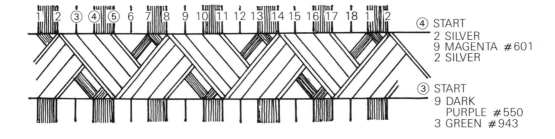

Thread your needle with a long length of DARK PURPLE thread #550.

Beginning just to the LEFT of the last 2 silver rows (at the 3):
>   Do 9 DARK PURPLE (#550) ROWS.
>   Do 3 GREEN (#943) ROWS.

MOVE the START PIN to the NUMBER 1
position on the chart (Fig. 26), just to the
LEFT of the LIGHT PURPLE #554 section.

Fig. 26

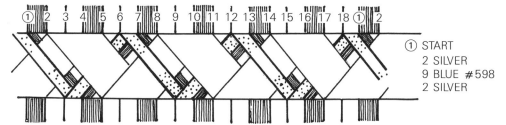

① START
2 SILVER
9 BLUE #598
2 SILVER

Thread your needle with SILVER.
Do 2 ROWS of SILVER following the
OVER/UNDER PATTERN in Figure 26.

REMEMBER:
    Put the needle UNDER EYE-END FIRST.
    Be sure the needle doesn't catch any stray
    threads on the way through.

Fig. 27

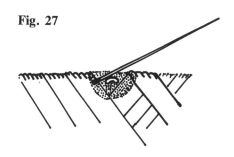

Following the SAME OVER/UNDER PATTERN:
    Do 9 ROWS in BLUE #598
    Do 2 ROWS in SILVER.

This completes the Obi pattern.

If little corners of the paper show (those that
are not covered), use the EYE-END of your
needle to push the areas of paper underneath
the Obi thread layer. Your basting stitches will
disappear into the ball's thread wrap. (Fig. 27)

THE SILVER CRISS-CROSS STITCH:

At the NORTH POLE END of the ball, select
the 3 SECTIONS (of the six in between the
silver stripes) which DO NOT HAVE A
NOTCH in the OBI's EDGE. (Fig. 28)
These 3 SECTIONS will be used for the
CRISS-CROSS stitch made with the SILVER
MARKING THREAD.

With your PAPER STRIP, use the 18th
MEASUREMENTS.

Divide the FIRST 18th MEASUREMENT into
HALF.

Fig. 28

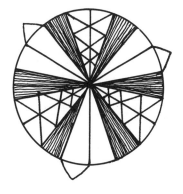

Fig. 29

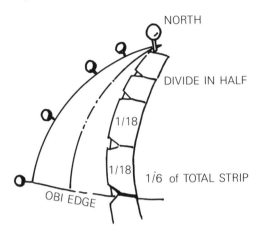

NORTH

DIVIDE IN HALF

1/18

1/18

1/6 of TOTAL STRIP

OBI EDGE

BEGIN at the BOTTOM (the TOP EDGE of the OBI THREADS).

INSERT 4 pins on EACH SIDE of the section. (Fig. 29)

ENTER your needle so that it EXITS at the TOP LEFT PIN. (Fig. 30)

Use the Basic Stitch and make a ZIG-ZAG line following the NUMBERS 1—4 in Figure 31.

Close the zig-zag line by carrying the thread UNDER the ball's surface from NUMBERS 4 to 5 at the Obi Edge.

Fig. 30

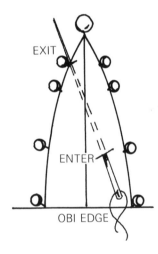

EXIT

ENTER

OBI EDGE

Fig. 31

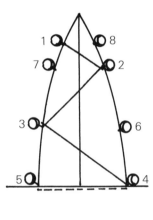

1   8
7   2

3   6

5   4

Fig. 32

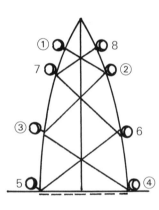

①   8
7   ②

③   6

5   ④

Fig. 33

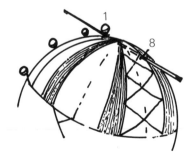

1

8

Follow the NUMBERS 5 to 8 to complete the Criss-Cross stitch. (Fig. 32)

As you ENTER at 8, EXIT your needle at the TOP LEFT PIN in the next section to be stitched. (Fig. 33)

REPEAT the CRISS-CROSS stitch in the 3 SECTIONS WITHOUT NOTCHES at the SOUTH POLE end.

The ball is complete.

BALL #9 "Chrysanthemum"

This ball is traditionally known as the KIKU or chrysanthemum pattern. Stitching on alternating division threads creates this kaleidoscoping design. By changing the number of division lines around the OBI, the width of the "petals" will change. Fewer divisions around the OBI make wider "petals". Experiment with different numbers on subsequent balls!

MATERIALS:

One 4 inch ball, thread wrap in deep turquoise
    (to match DMC #943 as closely as possible)

DMC Pearl Cotton #5 in 6 colors:
    Orange #741
    Yellow-Orange #742
    Yellow #743
    White #5
    Dark Green #943
    Medium Purple #552

Silver marking thread

Two Needles

Paper strip for marking

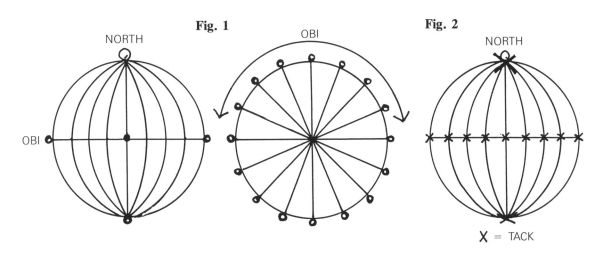

Fig. 1

Fig. 2

X = TACK

MEASURE THE BALL into SIXTEENTHS around the OBI LINE. (Fig. 1)

TACK the NORTH and SOUTH POLE threads. TACK EACH INTERSECTION around the Obi Line. (Fig. 2)
REMOVE the PINS from the Obi Line when tacking is complete.

Divide 1/4 of your paper measure into
THIRDS. (Fig. 3)

Fig. 3

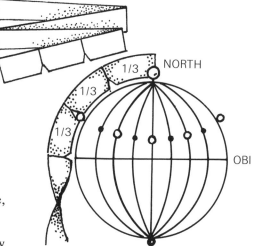

On EACH OF THE 16 DIVISION LINES,
measure 2/3 of the way DOWN from the
NORTH POLE to the OBI line and MARK
this 2/3 measurement with a pin.

Use 2 colors of pins, such as yellow and blue,
alternating the color on every other line.

Measure only the NORTH end now, too many
pins get in the way.

Fig. 4

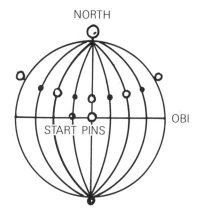

Insert 2 extra START PINS at the OBI LINE,
a yellow pin on one yellow division line, a
blue pin on the blue division line to the LEFT
of it. (Fig. 4)
The start pins will help you to START and
END at the SAME PLACE each time.

Fig. 5

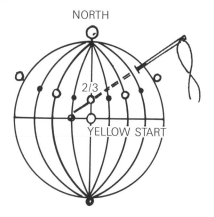

Thread your needle with a long length of
ORANGE thread #741.

ENTER your needle so that it EXITS just
below the 2/3 measurement pin at the
YELLOW START LINE. (Fig. 5)

Pull the thread through until the end
disappears below the surface of the ball.

Fig. 6

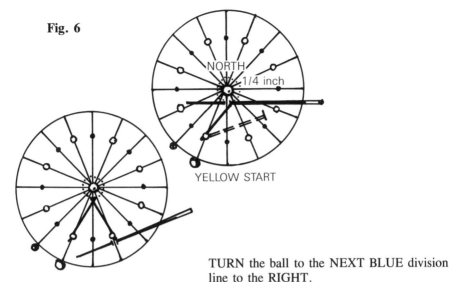

YELLOW START

Fig. 7

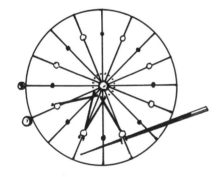

TURN the ball to the NEXT BLUE division line to the RIGHT.

Take a stitch under the division line 1/4 INCH DOWN from the North Pole pin. (Fig. 6)

TURN the ball one more division line to the RIGHT. Take a stitch BELOW the YELLOW 2/3 mark pin. (Fig. 7)

On the next BLUE division line take a stitch 1/4 INCH down from the NORTH POLE.

On the next YELLOW division line take a stitch BELOW the 2/3 mark pin.

IMPORTANT:
As you continue, KEEP the STITCHES that are near the NORTH POLE EXACTLY 1/4 INCH out from the North Pole Pin. This will create a circle around the North Pole Pin that is 1/2 INCH in DIAMETER.

Fig. 8

Continue around the ball creating a star-shape until you return to the YELLOW START PIN.

Complete the final stitch BELOW the 2/3 MARK at the YELLOW START.

Stitch the needle into the ball near the YELLOW START PIN to hold it while using your second needle. (Fig. 8)

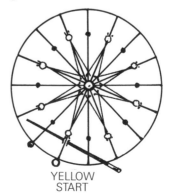

YELLOW START

Fig. 9

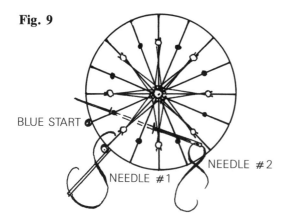

BLUE START

NEEDLE #2

NEEDLE #1

Fig. 10

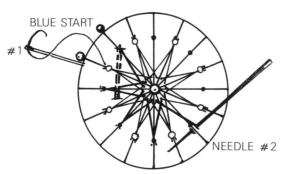

BLUE START

#1

NEEDLE #2

This pattern alternates back and forth from the "YELLOW START" to the "BLUE START" until its completion.

THREAD your SECOND NEEDLE with the SAME COLOR orange thread #741.

ENTER the needle so that it EXITS just BELOW the 2/3 MARK PIN on the BLUE START LINE to the LEFT. (Fig. 9)

With the second needle make the EXACT SAME PATTERN of stitches on the OPPOSITE MARKS. (This time all the yellow line stitches will be up near the North Pole and the BLUE line stitches will be down at the 2/3 MARK.) (Fig. 10)

This new pattern goes ON TOP of the first.

END at the BLUE START PIN by completing the FIRST STITCH BELOW the 2/3 MARK and inserting the second needle into the ball near the BLUE START PIN.

Fig. 11

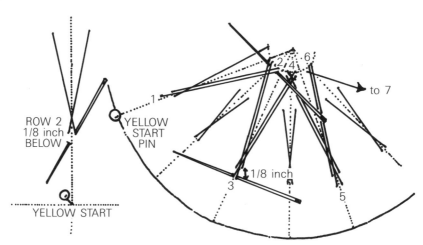

ROW 2
1/8 inch
BELOW

YELLOW
START
PIN

1

to 7

3

1/8 inch

5

YELLOW START

BEGIN again at the YELLOW START PIN with NEEDLE #1 and the same ORANGE thread #741. Make the SECOND ROW of stitches lie JUST BELOW the first row, both around the North Pole and at the 2/3 MARKS. (Fig. 11)

Continue around the ball.
Complete the second orange row of the beginning stitch.

ESCAPE the ORANGE thread #741 and NEEDLE #1.

Fig. 12

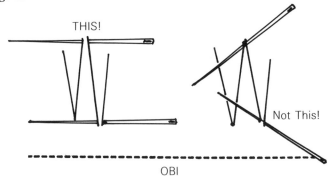

THIS!

Not This!

OBI

As you continue, take each stitch with your needle HORIZONTAL and PARALLEL to the OBI LINE. (Fig. 12)

Fig. 13

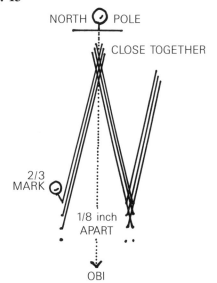

NORTH POLE

CLOSE TOGETHER

2/3 MARK

1/8 inch APART

OBI

KEEP the STITCHES that are near the NORTH POLE spaced very CLOSELY TOGETHER. They will move down because of the tension. (Fig. 13)

SPACE the STITCHES near the OBI LINE 1/8 INCH APART. They will move up.

BEGIN at the BLUE START PIN with NEEDLE #2:

Do a SECOND ROW with the ORANGE thread #741.

ESCAPE the ORANGE thread #741 and NEEDLE #2.

REMOVE the 2/3 MARK PINS.

Fig. 14

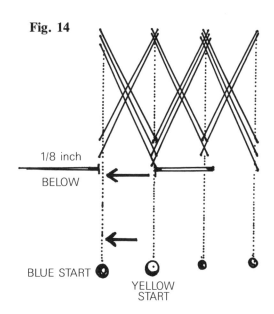

1/8 inch

BELOW

BLUE START

YELLOW START

NOTE: For the next 2 rows we will use just 1 ROW of each color. With 1 ROW of color around each START it is easier to use ONE NEEDLE with enough thread for BOTH STARTS. (Fig. 14)

Using the YELLOW-ORANGE thread #742:
  Do 1 ROW beginning at the YELLOW START,
  Do 1 ROW beginning at the BLUE START.
  ESCAPE the YELLOW-ORANGE thread #742.

Using the YELLOW thread #743:
  Do 1 ROW beginning at the YELLOW START,
  Do 1 ROW beginning at the BLUE START.
  ESCAPE the YELLOW thread #743.

NOTE: You will see that your stitches up near the NORTH POLE are becoming WIDER as the needle passes UNDER the DIVISION LINE and the PREVIOUS ROWS—LET THEM become wider. Don't try to pull them back into a straight, narrow line. Allow this widening to take place GRADUALLY as the stitches progress downward. (Fig. 15)

AGAIN USE 2 NEEDLES, each threaded with a long length of WHITE thread #5.

Begin the FIRST at the YELLOW START.
ENTER the needle so that it EXITS 1/8 INCH BELOW the LAST yellow stitch.
Do this row around the ball.
Complete the LAST stitch and LEAVE NEEDLE #1 at the YELLOW START PIN.

Fig. 15

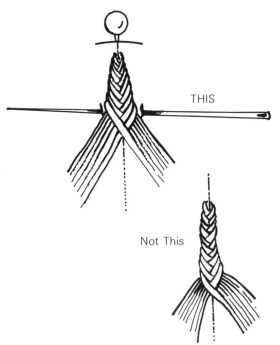

THIS

Not This

With NEEDLE #2 begin at the BLUE START, 1/8 INCH BELOW the last row.
Do 1 ROW of WHITE #5.
Go to the YELLOW START, do 1 ROW of WHITE #5.
Go to the BLUE START, do 1 ROW of WHITE #5.

Fig. 16

Continue ALTERNATING the WHITE (#5) ROWS one at a time until 7 ROWS have been completed from the YELLOW START and 7 ROWS have been completed from the BLUE START.

To give yourself more room for stitches at the TOP, use the EYE-END of your needle to PULL DOWN the crossed threads in the CENTER of each point of the star. (Fig. 16)

Upon completion, the WHITE POINTS should extend to 1/4 INCH ABOVE THE OBI LINE. (Fig. 17)

To complete the NORTH POLE PATTERN.
    Do 1 ROW of SILVER from the YELLOW START,
    Do 1 ROW of SILVER from the BLUE START.
    ESCAPE the SILVER.

REPEAT the PATTERN IDENTICALLY at the SOUTH POLE END.

THE OBI LINE:

A simple WRAPPED OBI completes this ball.

REMEMBER:
Begin to wrap NEXT TO the Obi Line and WORK TOWARD the POLES.

Using PURPLE #552, do 4 WRAPS ABOVE the OBI MARK LINE and 4 WRAPS BELOW the Obi mark line. (Fig. 18)

Do 3 WRAPS of GREEN #943 on EACH SIDE, outside the purple lines.

Do 2 more PURPLE (#552) WRAPS on each side outside the green lines.

The ball is complete.

Fig. 17

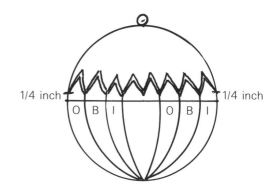

1/4 inch   1/4 inch

O B I   O B I

Fig. 18

2 PURPLE #552	
3 GREEN #943	
4 PURPLE #552	
OBI	
4 PURPLE #552	
3 GREEN #943	
2 PURPLE #552	

EGG #1 "Princess's Crown"

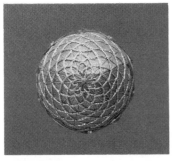

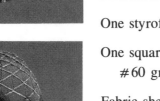

The decorated egg, a decidedly Western tradition, can be interpreted with effective results using TEMARI stitching techniques.

Because the egg's form is not totally symmetrical, as is a sphere, the preparation of the form's covering and the materials have, by necessity, been modified. Measuring and stitching techniques are basically the same.

MATERIALS:

One styrofoam egg blank, 5 inches tall

One square yard of gauze (CHEESECLOTH)
  #60 grade Cotton Gauze tightly woven (Fig. 1)

Fabric shears — sharp

One ball of DMC Pearl Cotton #5, Yellow #744
  for surface covering

DMC Pearl Cotton #5 in 6 colors:
  Dark Blue #806
  Peach #352
  Orange #350
  Yellow-Orange #742
  Maroon #814
  White #5

Gold marking thread

Regular sewing thread — Yellow to match DMC #744

Two paper strips

Centimeter tape measure

Fig. 1

—— WRAPPING THE EGG ——

TO BEGIN, fold your square yard of cheesecloth DIAGONALLY. (Fig. 2)

With your fabric shears, CUT along the DIAGONAL FOLD.

Fig. 2

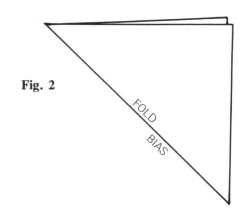

FOLD

BIAS

With the two halves together, cut BIAS STRIPS of cheesecloth that are 1-1/2 INCHES WIDE. (Fig. 3)

Cut enough BIAS STRIPS to TOTAL 10 YARDS laid end to end. (Fig. 4)

These BIAS STRIPS will be WRAPPED OVER the styrofoam egg shape. They will TAKE the PLACE of the BATTING layer, the YARN WRAP layer and the THREAD WRAP layer that is used on the TEMARI.

BEGIN by wrapping the SHORTEST cheesecloth strips from top to bottom LENGTHWISE around the egg.

WRAP TIGHTLY.

As you wrap each bias strip, MOULD it to the egg with your HANDS so that the edges of each strip lie flat against the egg. (Fig. 5)

Fig. 3

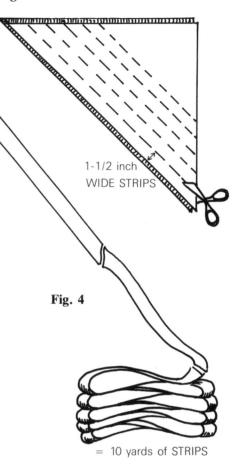

1-1/2 inch
WIDE STRIPS

Fig. 4

= 10 yards of STRIPS

Fig. 5

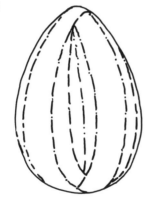

Fig. 6

Next WRAP strips DIAGONALLY around the egg. Continue MOULDING the EDGES to the egg shape as you wrap. (Fig. 6)

COVER the egg EVENLY:
    WATCH for LUMPS (too many crossvers).
    WATCH for FLAT SPOTS (not enough coverage).

WRAP ALL of the STRIPS onto the egg. USE ALL 10 YARDS.

The gauze does NOT need to be stitched on. Simply wrap it on SMOOTHLY and TIGHTLY, making sure there are NO WRINKLES.

— DIVIDING THE EGG —

Check the surface for lumps and flat spots before dividing. Push down on lumps to flatten them. If necessary wrap more gauze over flat spots.

Carefully LOCATE the NORTH POLE at the TOP point of the egg. Be sure it is in the center. (Fig. 7)
This can only be done by trial and error and by looking carefully and turning the egg around, viewing the silhouette.

With ONE paper strip find the SOUTH POLE. SAVE your STRIP.

Fig. 7

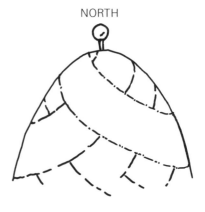

NORTH

The OBI LINE will be located at the WIDEST circumference of the egg. This is NOT the MIDDLE from top to bottom. (Fig. 8)

Place 5 to 6 PINS around the WIDEST CIRCUMFERENCE WHERE YOU THINK the OBI SHOULD BE. Again use the egg's silhouette.

Fig. 8

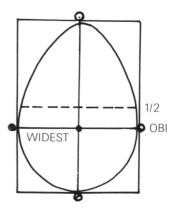

1/2

OBI

WIDEST

Fig. 9

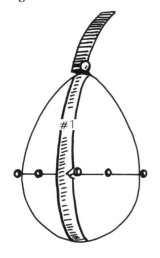

#1

Measure with your #1 paper strip to the pins. PLACE them all on the SAME OBI LINE around the egg. (Fig. 9)

Fig. 10

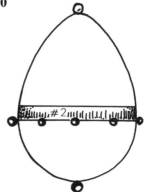

#2

With a SECOND PAPER STRIP, measure AROUND the OBI LINE to find its circumference. (Fig. 10)

Fig. 11

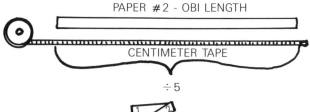

PAPER #2 - OBI LENGTH

CENTIMETER TAPE

÷5

FOLD

Fig. 12

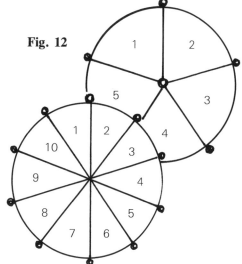

DIVIDE the OBI MEASUREMENT into FIFTHS. This is most easily done by measuring the paper strip and egg around the Obi with your CENTIMETER TAPE MEASURE.

Measure the distance around the fattest part of the egg.

DIVIDE this number by 5. (Fig.11)

FOLD your #2 paper into 5 EQUAL PARTS. Place pins at 1/5 divisions around the Obi Line. (Fig. 12)

Divide the FIFTHS in HALF so that the Obi is divided into TENTHS.

CHECK your OBI LINE with PAPER STRIP #1.

With your matching yellow sewing thread, mark the egg into TENTHS with an OBI.

TACK the NORTH and SOUTH POLE threads. (Fig. 13)

TACK the OBI Line INTERSECTIONS.

Fig. 13   TACK

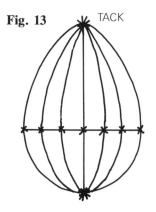

Fig. 14

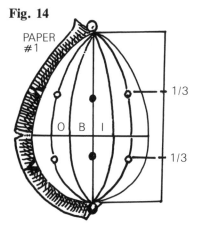

PAPER #1

1/3

O B I

1/3

Using PAPER STRIP #1, divide EVERY OTHER line into THIRDS (disregard the Obi Line for this measurement). (Fig. 14)

Place a pin at the THIRD MARKS on EVERY OTHER division line.

SAVE YOUR PAPER STRIPS!

THE THREAD COVER:

A layer of Pearl Cotton thread will now be applied over the gauze wrap layer. The Pearl Cotton will be applied using the basic stitch and in the very same way as the pattern on BALL #1. The five petal-shaped panels around the egg use the 1/3 MARK PINS AS THEIR CENTERS.

TO BEGIN thread your needle with a long length of YELLOW #744.

Fig. 15

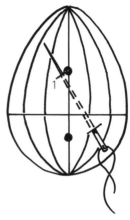

Fig. 16

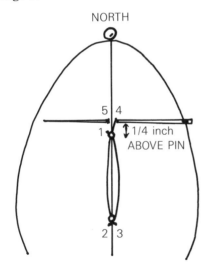

Fig. 17

ENTER your needle so that it EXITS just to the LEFT of one UPPER 1/3 MARK PIN. (Fig. 15)

Pull the thread through until the end disappears deep beneath the gauze surface.

As in Ball #1, carry the thread around the TOP of the UPPER PIN. TURN the egg so that the SOUTH POLE is now on TOP. (Fig. 16)

Take a tiny stitch under the MARK LINE, above the PIN.

TURN the egg—NORTH on TOP. Take a tiny stitch 1/4 INCH ABOVE the PIN. (Fig. 17)

TURN the egg—SOUTH on TOP. Take a stitch 1/4 INCH ABOVE the LAST. (Fig. 18)

Fig. 18

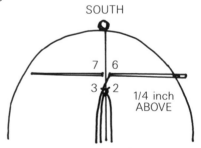

Pull the first 6 to 8 rows fairly tight so that they lay flat against the surface.

Fig. 19

CLOSE TOGETHER

CLOSE TOGETHER

The SPACING of the stitches is very IMPORTANT on the egg-shape. (Fig. 19)

In the area just above and below the PINS where the form is LESS CURVED, the stitches must be placed FARTHER APART (1/4 INCH apart to begin, then 1/8 INCH apart for about the first inch above and below the pins).

As the form's curve becomes more pronounced top and bottom, stitches should be placed closer together, NO SPACE IN BETWEEN.

Fig. 20

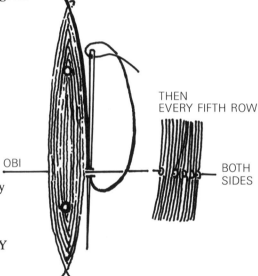

OBI

THEN EVERY FIFTH ROW

BOTH SIDES

When 6 to 8 rows have been completed a tiny TACK STITCH around the Obi Mark Line holds the threads in place. (Fig. 20)

Do a TACK STITCH at the Obi Line EVERY FIFTH ROW until the panel is complete.

Fig. 21

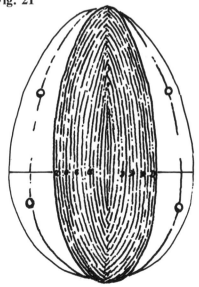

The panel is complete when threads cover a FIFTH DIVISION from the TENTH LINE on the RIGHT to the TENTH LINE on the LEFT and stitches reach from the NORTH POLE PIN to the SOUTH POLE PIN. (Fig. 21)

Continue around the ball untill ALL 5 PANELS are completed. Add extra threads to fill in bare spots if necessary.

109

── DECORATING THE EGG ──

Using your PAPER STRIP #1,

RELOCATE with your paper measures and pins:
1. the NORTH POLE
2. the SOUTH POLE
3. the OBI LINE
4. the 10 DIVISION LINES

Fig. 22

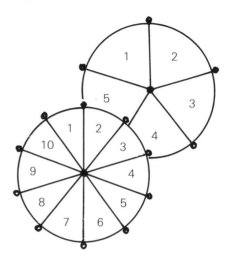

Fig. 23

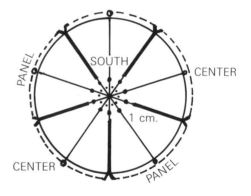

THE NET STITCH:

The Net Stitch is applied over the thread cover layer. It is applied from the South Pole to the Obi Line and from the North Pole to the Obi Line.

Using the obvious division lines provided by the 5 thread cover panels' centers and sides, MEASURE 1 CENTIMETER DOWN from the SOUTH POLE PIN on each of the 10 division lines. (Fig. 24)

Measure ONE HALF (1/2) CENTIMETER down from the South Pole pin in between each tenth. DON'T MARK WITH PINS, too many pins get in the way.

Thread your needle with about 24 inches of GOLD marking thread. KNOT the thread's END.

ENTER your needle BETWEEN THREADS so that it EXITS just to the LEFT of one of the 1/2 centimeter points. (Fig. 25)
Pull the end through carefully so that the knot disappears under the thread cover.

Fig. 24

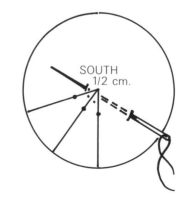

Fig. 25

Fig. 26

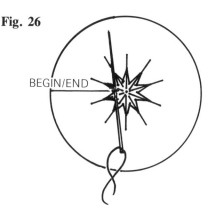

BEGIN/END

Fig. 27

NEW ROW

TACK
STITCH

STITCH a 10-POINTED STAR around the South Pole pin using the 1/2 and 1 centimeter measurements. Remove the pins as you complete each stitch.

KEEP THE MEASUREMENTS ACCURATE. (Fig. 26)

COMPLETE the FINAL stitch.

Fig. 28

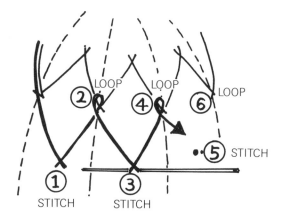

FIRST ROW

TACK

② LOOP

① STITCH

CATCH GOLD THREAD ONLY

Fig. 29

LOOP   LOOP   LOOP
②   ④   ⑥
         ⑤ STITCH
① STITCH   ③ STITCH

Then CARRY the thread along the LEFT side of the "V" of the last stitch.
Take a tiny tack stitch at the bottom point of the "V." (Fig. 27)

To begin the next row:
Carry the thread down to the next division line on the RIGHT.

Take a stitch under the division line.

Then carry the thread up to the next point of the row above, moving to the RIGHT.

②LOOP: CATCH with the needle the LEFT SIDE gold thread of the "V" (Fig. 28) but DO NOT take a stitch into the egg's surface. Just LOOP the thread THROUGH the first row of thread at the LEFT side of the point.

FOR THE LOOP: pushing the eye-end of the needle through first instead of the point may avoid catching the thread.

Pull the LOOP tight.
Carry the thread over to the next division line to the RIGHT. (Fig. 29)
　　③ Take a STITCH UNDER the division line.
　　④ CARRY the thread up to the next point on the RIGHT and CATCH only the LEFT side thread. Pull the LOOP tight.

Fig. 30

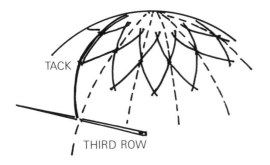

TACK

THIRD ROW

CONTINUE all the way around the egg until you END where you began.

To BEGIN the NEXT ROW, again CARRY the thread ALONGSIDE the first completed zig-zag and EXTEND the line down to the next division line on the RIGHT. (Fig. 30)

Fig. 31

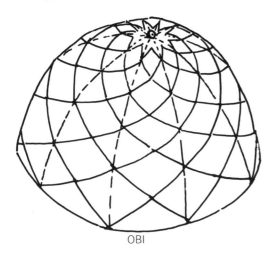

OBI

Each time you begin a NEW ROW, gradually LENGTHEN the space inside the diamonds, making each row of diamonds slightly larger than the last. (Fig. 31)

Continue the NET STITCH all the way to the OBI MARK LINE.

Fig. 32

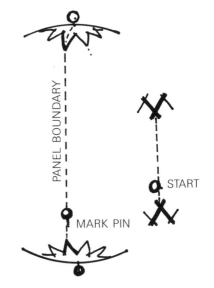

PANEL BOUNDARY

START

MARK PIN

TURN the egg so the NORTH POLE is at the TOP.

Choose a starting place for the North Pole side by returning to the South Pole and selecting a MARK LINE that has a first row STITCH pointing to the NORTH POLE. (Fig. 32)

Follow that mark line to the NORTH POLE and MARK it with a pin. Use that mark line to begin your first North Pole row.

Fig. 33

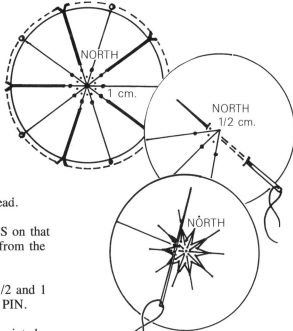

Thread your needle with GOLD thread.

ENTER your needle so that it EXITS on that MARK LINE, 1/2 (0.5) centimeter from the North Pole pin.

Do the FIRST ROW of ZIG-ZAG 1/2 and 1 centimeter from the NORTH POLE PIN. (Fig. 33)
As with the South Pole, stitch a 10-pointed star around the North Pole pin.

Fig. 34

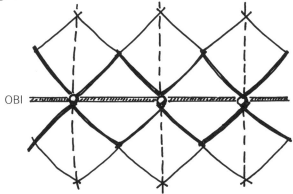

Continue the NET STITCH so that it COVERS the egg down to the OBI.

At the Obi, the diamonds points should meet. (Fig. 34)

SPACE your NET ROWS so that they come as close to the OBI as possible.

If the points do not meet exactly at the OBI line, don't worry. The Obi pattern will cover the gap.

THE OBI PATTERN:

Use your paper measure to RELOCATE your OBI MARK LINE and mark it with GOLD thread.

Fig. 35

Again with GOLD thread
>   Do 5 WRAPS of GOLD
>   ABOVE the Obi.
>   Do 5 WRAPS of GOLD
>   BELOW the Obi. (Fig. 35)

Escape the GOLD.

Fig. 36

RELOCATE the 10 INTERSECTIONS around the Obi Line, the centers and outside boundaries of each panel.

Insert KEEPER PINS on EVERY OTHER tenth mark line around the Obi. The FIVE sets of keeper pins around the Obi can be located at the boundary of each panel.

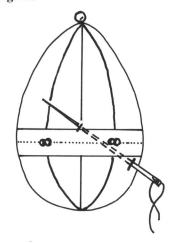

Measure 7 WRAPS of BLUE #806 and thread your needle.

Hold the egg will the NORTH POLE at the TOP.

Fig. 37

ENTER your needle so that it EXITS just ABOVE the Obi gold rows, at a DIVISION LINE WITHOUT KEEPER PINS. (Fig. 36)

Pull the thread through so that the end disappears beneath the egg's surface.

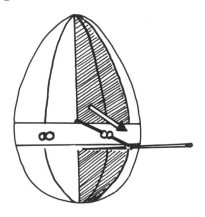

Fig. 38

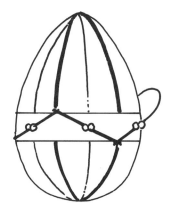

Carry the thread through the KEEPER PINS on the RIGHT.

Take a STITCH just BELOW the GOLD Obi rows on the next tenth division line to the RIGHT. (Fig. 37)

TURN the egg to the LEFT.
Take a stitch ABOVE the GOLD Obi. (Fig. 38)

Fig. 39

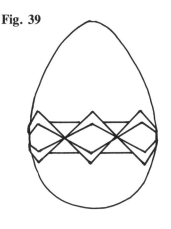

CONTINUE around the Obi making a ZIG-ZAG line until DIAMONDS with 3 ROWS of BLUE #806 ABOVE the Obi and 3 ROWS BELOW the Obi are completed.
(Fig. 39)

Using the PEACH thread #352,
   do 5 ROWS of PEACH #352
   outside the blue.

Using the ORANGE thread #350,
   do 3 ROWS outside the peach. (Fig. 40)
Do 2 ROWS of YELLOW-ORANGE #742.
Do 2 ROWS of GOLD.
Do 1 ROW of MAROON #814.

Thread your needle with Blue thread #806. ENTER your needle deeply so that it EXITS just above the cluster of threads between 2 keeper pins. (Fig. 41)

Pull the thread through.
Take 6 to 8 stitches VERTICALLY around the thread cluster. (Fig. 42)
Try not to catch the gold Obi rows.

Escape the thread and go on to the next until all 5 clusters have been completed.

The first half of the Obi pattern is complete.

Fig. 40

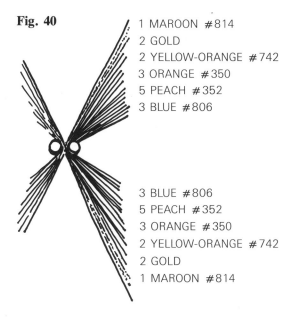

1 MAROON #814
2 GOLD
2 YELLOW-ORANGE #742
3 ORANGE #350
5 PEACH #352
3 BLUE #806

3 BLUE #806
5 PEACH #352
3 ORANGE #350
2 YELLOW-ORANGE #742
2 GOLD
1 MAROON #814

Fig. 41

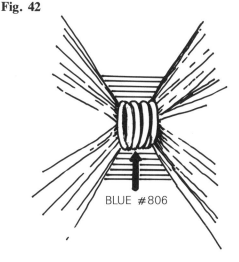

Fig. 42

BLUE #806

115

Fig. 43

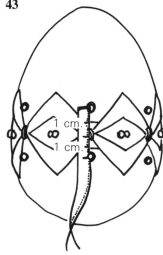

Move your keeper pins to the CENTER of each DIAMOND that has been completed. (Fig. 43)

With your centimeter tape, measure
1 centimeter UP from the OBI line and
1 centimeter DOWN from the Obi on each
division line with a blue knot.
This measurement is the starting place for the second half of the Obi Pattern.

Fig. 44

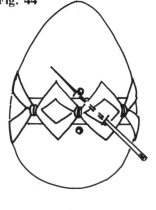

Fig. 45

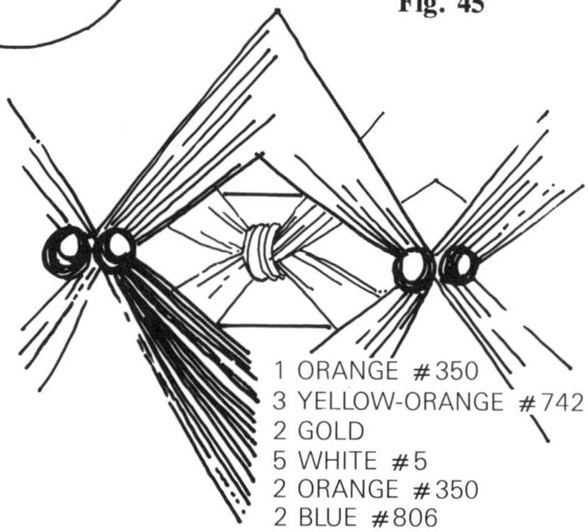

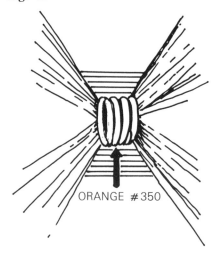

Thread your needle with ORANGE #350.

ENTER your needle so that it EXITS just to the LEFT of a 1 centimeter pin ABOVE the Obi. (Fig. 44)

1 ORANGE #350
3 YELLOW-ORANGE #742
2 GOLD
5 WHITE #5
2 ORANGE #350
2 BLUE #806
2 GOLD

Do 1 ROW of ORANGE #350 ABOVE and BELOW the Obi. (Fig. 45)

Do 3 ROWS of YELLOW-ORANGE #742 outside the orange.

Fig. 46

Do 2 ROWS of GOLD outside the yellow-orange.

Do 5 ROWS of WHITE #5 outside the gold.

Do 2 ROWS of ORANGE #350 outside the white.

Do 2 ROWS of BLUE #806 outside the orange.

Do 2 ROWS of GOLD outside the blue.

Use the ORANGE thread #350 to STITCH the CLUSTERS of threads between the keeper pins. (Fig. 46)

The egg is complete.

ORANGE #350

EGG #2 "Rippling River"

MATERIALS:

One styrofoam egg blank, 4 inches tall

One square yard of gauze (#60 cheesecloth)

DMC Pearl Cotton #5 in 2 colors:
    Medium Purple #552 for covering
    Yellow-Orange #742

Gold marking thread

Silver marking thread

Regular sewing thread — Purple (same color as DMC #552)

Two paper strips

Tissue paper

Two needles

COVER the styrofoam egg blank with 10 yards of gauze strips.

MEASURE the egg into TENTHS with an OBI LINE around the widest circumference.

Use your PURPLE REGULAR SEWING THREAD to MARK the egg.

Fig. 1

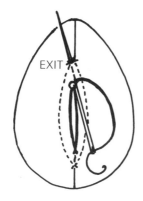

EXIT

THE THREAD COVER:

The thread cover uses a pattern of ONE row of GOLD between every FIVE rows of PURPLE.

In each panel there are FIVE GOLD LINES and FOUR PURPLE SPACES.

The THIRD GOLD LINE of each panel equals a 20TH DIVISION MEASUREMENT. Check your accuracy and spacing as you proceed.

Thread one of your needles with about ONE YARD of GOLD thread.

KNOT the thread's end.

ENTER the needle so that it EXITS Just to the LEFT of the UPPER 1/3 MARK PIN.

Do the FIRST ROW in the CENTER of the panel with GOLD, then EXIT the gold thread about 1/2 INCH UP the division line to be ready for the next gold row. (Fig. 1)

117

Thread your SECOND needle with a long length of PURPLE thread.

Do 5 ROWS of PURPLE outside the gold.

Do 1 ROW of GOLD outside the 5 purple rows. (Fig. 2)

Do 5 ROWS of PURPLE.
Do a TACK STITCH at the Obi Mark Line in EACH PURPLE SECTION.

Do 1 ROW of GOLD.
Now check your SPACING to make sure that this GOLD ROW lies at a TWENTIETH DIVISION mark on each side of the center.

Do 5 ROWS of PURPLE.

Do 1 ROW of GOLD.

Do 5 ROWS of PURPLE.

Do 1 ROW of GOLD.

The panel is complete.

COMPLETE the FOUR remaining PANELS in this way.

Where the panels meet there will be 2 ROWS of GOLD together. (Fig. 3)

THE OBI:

The obi design for this egg is based on the same principle as the obi design on Ball #8. To refresh your memory, go back to Ball #8 and review the instructions for the obi.

As in Ball #8, cut a strip of tissue paper, this one 1 INCH WIDE and LONG enough to wrap around the OBI MARK LINE with an overlap of 1/2 INCH.

MEASURE and CUT the tissue strip ACCURATELY, this is your guideline.

Fig. 2

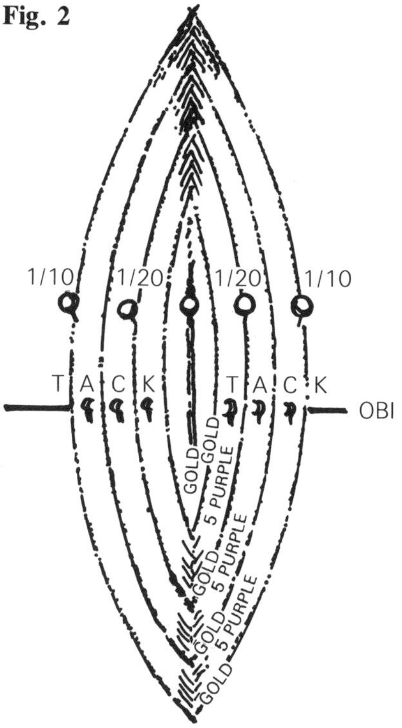

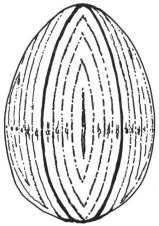

Fig. 3

RELOCATE your OBI MARK LINE with your paper measuring strip.

MARK with pins an accurate Obi Line.

FOLD your TISSUE paper strip in HALF LENGTHWISE. (Fig. 4)

Fig. 4

FOLD ▶

Fig. 5

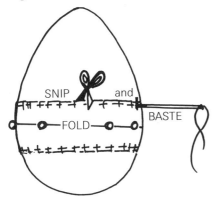

SNIP and

FOLD

BASTE

LAY the FOLD of the TISSUE strip on TOP of the OBI MARK LINE.

PIN the strip accurately around the egg at the Obi Mark Line.

CLIP the EDGES TOP and BOTTOM with your scissors so that they will lie flat against the egg. (Fig. 5)

Using your REGULAR PURPLE SEWING THREAD, BASTE the strip to the egg as near to the edges as possible.

Now using the DMC YELLOW-ORANGE #742, MEASURE 6 WRAPS plus 5 INCHES.

Thread your needle.

ENTER your needle so that it EXITS at the OBI Mark Line, the FOLD LINE on the tissue paper. (Fig. 6)

Fig. 6

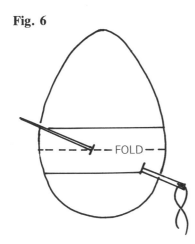

FOLD

Fig. 7

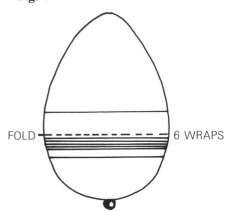

FOLD — — — — — 6 WRAPS

WRAP 6 ROWS of YELLOW-ORANGE #742 from the Obi line toward the SOUTH POLE on TOP of the tissue paper Obi. ALIGN the threads closely next to each other. (Fig. 7)

Fig. 8

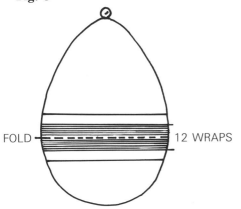

FOLD — 12 WRAPS

MEASURE another 6 WRAPS plus 5 INCHES of YELLOW-ORANGE #742.

WRAP 6 MORE ROWS from the OBI line toward the NORTH POLE. (Fig. 8), for a total of 12 ROWS of YELLOW-ORANGE thread #742 wrapped around the center of the tissue paper Obi.

ESCAPE the YELLOW-ORANGE thread #742.
Remove the pins around the obi.

Fig. 9

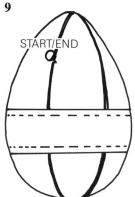

START/END

THE DIAMOND PATTERN:

For the pattern one Obi pattern stitch will be taken on each vertical thread of the thread cover.

Each time you take a stitch catch a little of the gauze wrap and one vertical thread of the thread cover. The gauze wrap will help to hold the vertical threads in place as you progress around the Obi.

Fig. 10

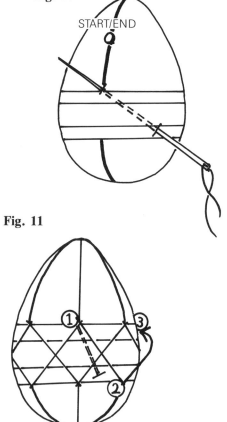

START/END

Place a RED PIN at one PANEL'S EDGE to MARK your START and END Place.

Keep another colored pin handy to mark your ending when you run out of thread. (Fig. 9)

Thread your needle with about 1 YARD of PURPLE thread #552.

ENTER your needle so that it EXITS at the TOP of the TISSUE Obi and just to the LEFT of the TWO GOLD threads of the panel's boundaries. (Fig. 10)

Fig. 11

The first purple thread (#552) row will ZIG-ZAG around the Obi, placing a stitch above and below the Obi tissue on the double GOLD thread boundary lines of the 5 panels. Catch BOTH GOLD threads in each stitch.
Do 1 ROW of PURPLE diamonds around the egg, over the yellow-orange center rows. (Fig. 11)

ESCAPE the thread into the tissue Obi area.

Fig. 12

As in Ball #8, each row will be placed to the LEFT of the one before. (Fig. 12)

ZIG-ZAG stitching will move around the egg to the RIGHT.

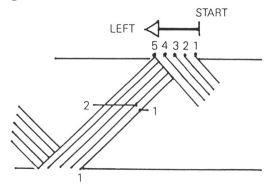

This pattern progresses from the outside RIGHT panel boundary to the CENTER line in each panel.

Thread your needle with about 1 YARD of GOLD thread.

DO NOT use long lengths of metallic threads when stitching your design. Metallics tend to become snarled and unravel. Use SHORTER pieces and rethread your needle MORE OFTEN.

ENTER your needle so that it EXITS to the LEFT of the FIRST PURPLE thread #552, on the LEFT of the gold panel boundary where you began. (Fig. 13)

On the 5 VERTICAL threads of the thread cover, do 5 ROWS of GOLD diamonds around the Obi. (Fig. 14)

At the GOLD VERTICAL thread to the LEFT, do 1 ROW of PURPLE (#552) diamonds.

On the 5 PURPLE VERTICAL threads #552 to the LEFT, do 5 ROWS of SILVER diamonds.

At the GOLD VERTICAL thread, do 1 ROW of PURPLE (#552) diamonds.

On the 5 PURPLE threads #552, do 5 GOLD ROWS. (Fig. 15)

On the 1 GOLD VERTICAL thread, do 1 PURPLE (#552) ROW.

Fig. 13

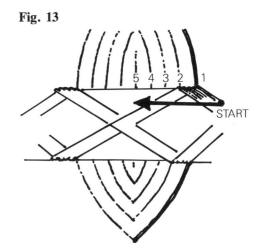

Fig. 14

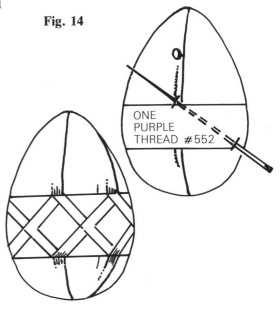

ONE PURPLE THREAD #552

Fig. 15

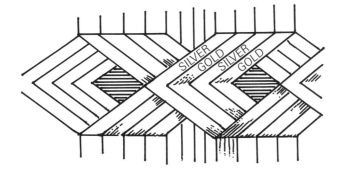

On the 5 PURPLE threads #552, do 5 SILVER ROWS.

On the FINAL GOLD thread in the CENTER of the panel, do 1 PURPLE (#552) ROW.

To complete the egg, use the EYE-END of your needle to PUSH the tissue paper that is still visible back underneath the Obi pattern threads.

The egg is complete.

Bibliography

Bredon, Juliet and Mitrophanow, Igor; THE MOON YEAR, A RECORD OF CHINESE CUSTOMS AND FESTIVALS; Paragon Book Reprint Corp., New York, 1966. pp.394-395.

Joya, Mock; THINGS JAPANESE; Japanese News Service, Ltd., Tokyo, Japan, 1960.

Kaemmerer, Eric; TRADES AND CRAFTS OF OLD JAPAN, LEAVES FROM A CONTEMPORARY ALBUM; Charles E. Tuttle, Co., Tokyo, no date. pp.88-89.

Lee, Sherman E.; THE GENIUS OF JAPANESE DESIGN; Kodansha International, Tokyo, no date.

Munsterberg, Hugo; THE FOLK ARTS OF JAPAN; Charles E. Tuttle Co., Tokyo, no date. pp.21, 106.

Saint-Gilles, Amaury; MINGEI, JAPAN'S ENDURING FOLK ARTS; Amaury Saint-Gilles and John Wanamaker, Inc., Philadelphia, PA, 1983.

Sakamoto, Kazuya and Pomeroy, Charles; JAPANESE TOYS, PLAYING WITH HISTORY; Charles E. Tuttle, Co., Tokyo, 1965. pp.445, 450.

Smith, Bradley and Weng, Wan-go; CHINA: A HISTORY IN ART; Doubleday & Co., Inc., New York, no date. Figure 182.

Williams, C. A. S.; OUTLINES OF CHINESE SYMBOLISM AND ART MOTIVES; Dover Publications, Inc., New York, 1976. pp.253-255.

KODANSHA ENCYCLOPEDIA OF JAPAN; Kodansha Ltd., Tokyo, 1983.
    Volume 7, Page 381; "Temari History," article author: Saito Ryosuke.
    Volume 1, Page 148; "Otedama" (bean bags).
    Volume 4, Page 191; "Kemari," article authors: Inagaki, Shisei.

JAPAN, ITS LAND, PEOPLE AND CULTURE: compiled by the Japanese National Commission for UNESCO. Published by the Japanese Government Printing Bureau, Ministry of Finance, 1958.